ISBN 978-0-266-97440-6
PIBN 10917989

SEVENTH ANNUAL MEETING

OF THE

CENTRAL ASSOCIA

OF

.EORS AND SECONDARY SCHOOLS

Held at
Cleveland, Ohio, March 28 and 29, 1902

PROCEEDINGS

OF THE

SEVENTH ANNUAL MEETING

OF THE

NORTH CENTRAL ASSOCIATION

OF

COLLEGES AND SECONDARY SCHOOLS

Held at
Cleveland, Ohio, March 28 and 29, 1902

EDITED BY

FRED NEWTON SCOTT

SECRETARY OF THE ASSOCIATION

ANN ARBOR
PUBLISHED BY THE ASSOCIATION
1902

Copies of the Proceedings of the North Central Association of Colleges and Secondary Schools may be obtained by addressing the Treasurer of the Association, Mr. J. E. Armstrong, Englewood High School, Chicago. The price of single copies is twenty-five cents. The price of the complete set as far as published (eight numbers, including the Report of the Preliminary Meeting for Organization) is $1.50.

———

The next meeting of the Association will be held in Chicago, Friday and Saturday, April 3 and 4, 1903.

THE NORTH CENTRAL ASSOCIATION

OF

COLLEGES AND SECONDARY SCHOOLS.

———

The seventh annual meeting of the North Central Association of Colleges and Secondary Schools was held in the parlors of the Hollenden Hotel, Cleveland, Ohio, on Friday and Saturday, March 28 and 29, 1902.

———

FIRST SESSION, FRIDAY EVENING.

———

The Association was called to order at 10:30 a. m. by the President, Chancellor W. S. Chaplin, of Washington University. The address of welcome was given by Superintendent L. H. Jones, of Cleveland, who spoke as follows:

I esteem it an honor as well as a pleasure to be allowed to say to you just a word of greeting.

For seven years I have been allowed the privilege of paying my annual dues to this Association, and at every meeting have been present in spirit, but this is my first bodily appearance. It will therefore seem to you almost as if an outsider were giving you the word of welcome.

Indeed, Cleveland is proud to have you meet here. You are an Association which rarely meets away from its home, and when it does, it selects the best place. For that reason we are glad to have you here.

The constitution of this Association appears to be of the kind sure to advance education. It is never quite well, it seems to me, to have a body made up entirely of people with a common interest. Colleges and schools have certain fundamental principles that are common to the work of both, and yet there are certain marked differences. And I certainly believe it to be to our common good to look at these questions from different points. It is therefore fortunate for this body that we are composed of people from these different classes of schools.

Speaking at first entirely from the position of the public schools, I would say that, it seems to me, there would really be no difficulty at all in reaching a proper settlement of these questions of the secondary schools providing the college authorities at all times granted all that the secondary schools asked of them. I cannot take the time from your programme to discuss this question. This will perhaps be done at another time and place.

Now I think there is one thing to be done, and that is to charge both the secondary schools and colleges with one sin, which seems common to all, the tendency to teach subjects rather than students; and I believe that this may with propriety be charged more strongly against the colleges than the secondary schools. It seems to me that this is no small matter that the attention of the student should be strongly turned to the study of a single branch of learning without any attempt to see the relationship of that special branch to all others and to the conduct of life. I freely grant that it may sometimes be necessary for the sake of original research that some one should follow out one line of work; but in this case there is a return to such a person which partially makes up for the loss.

I even carry the idea so far that when a person applies to me for a position as teacher of Algebra, Latin, English, etc., I may say to him that we do not teach these subjects. That immediately raises a new question. Then I add that we have some most excellent teachers in our schools who use Algebra, Latin, English, etc., as a means of instruction, as a means of transfer of knowledge, but they do not teach these subjects,—they do teach pupils.

There is another question which will be brought before you today,—the matter of admission to the colleges. The day is coming, no matter what the college authorities say, when a graduate from the high school will not have to ask for admission to any college or University, but will find the door of all such wide open. And the question then will not be whether he can enter college, but whether he can stay in college.

I repeat that we cordially greet you and are glad to have you with us.

President Chaplin then delivered the annual address as follows:

EDUCATION AND SUCCESS.

To make a successful man four things are certainly necessary. There doubtless are other elements which may and do contribute to success, but these four I regard as essential. They are:

1. A certain amount of knowledge.
2. A certain mental training.
3. Fixed moral standards.
4. A set purpose.

What success is, what a successful man is, I will not attempt to define here; I will only say that to me the word carries with it an idea of service to one's fellowmen, individually and collectively. This success depends, I believe, on the four things named. There is no real success, no success which we can hold up to the young as a model, without them.

Accidental prominence, either from wealth, or advancement in politics, or from any other cause which has to be classed as exceptional and fortuitous, I exclude because we are looking for the causes which we can expect to command success.

It is one of our duties to mark the distinction between real and spurious success, between success which makes for the general good and that which is at the expense of and to the detriment of the public.

Now of these four, the first, "a certain amount of knowledge," is and has been provided by our educational institutions. It may, let us admit, be secured without their aid. But the progress through our schools is a much surer and more inexpensive way than any other. The self-taught man is a very valuable member of society. The trouble with him is that he is so rare, and that measuring the actual cost in time and effort to himself and to the community, he is expensive. How much more might such men as Abraham Lincoln have accomplished for themselves and others had they had the advantages of the schools of the present day, had they found the path to knowledge smoothed for their onward steps. Admitting fully that knowledge may be acquired without the schools, it would be idle to deny the value and efficiency of schooling in the making of successful men.

The second of the requisites for success which I have named, "a certain mental training," has not at all times received the attention which it deserved, but the characteristic educational feature of the present day is, I think, the prominence which is given to this training. We begin, at least begin, to see that any study pursued in the right way carries with it mental training; that the mind once trained to accurate thinking in any one subject will be likely to think accurately in regard to any other subject; and, consequently, that the individual choice of studies loses much of the importance which was once attached to it. The power to think accurately and quickly, again, can be and is acquired by many outside of our schools, through the hard knocks of practical experience. Indeed, I fear our schools will never excel the school of experience in some of its training. What body of scholars can equal the street boys in quickness or aptness of repartee? The course of training in our schools has advantages over the school of experience in that it is systematic and progressive, that it is always under kindly direction, and lastly and mainly, that its failures are not necessarily fatal.

The third point mentioned, "fixed moral standards," depends upon two other educational institutions besides the schools,—the home and the church. All these forces acting together are none too strong for the task before them. Whether on the whole they are succeeding or failing, whether our country is becoming more or less moral, is a question which cannot be answered with certainty. The statistics are imperfect and doubtful. As to the truth each one will have his impression, which will depend on his standpoint, and perhaps more still on his digestion or liver. But whatever the fact may be, the home, the church and the school are the forces which work for good in the struggle; and the school, I suspect, is, or can be made, the strongest force of the three. For, after all, in teaching morality example is more effective than precept, and I believe that our educational institutions as a whole offer the best models we have of right living and right thinking. The school, or college, or University which will tolerate a teacher who is in any way immoral is rare, extremely rare. To be for hours daily during the plastic years of one's life in contact with the class of people to which our teachers belong, is in itself a very great incentive to morality. To feel that one is incurring their displeasure and condemnation is a check to wrong doing. The opinion of the teachers is a safe, settled and kindly public opinion, acting in the most direct way. Whether it is possible to have more systematic teaching of morals in our schools is much debated, but not yet decided. I will not attempt to discuss the question here. But I may venture to say that to me it seems in every way desirable, and entirely practicable to lay much more stress on the teaching of morals than we do now. The discipline of our schools is by far the best discipline our young people receive.

To learn of the existence of superior authority, to be held to regular and satisfactory performance of tasks, to be made to recognize the rights of others, to be a part of a steadily moving organism, to be made to come and go at fixed times, is a great part of the training essential to good citizenship. In the schools these matters receive more attention than anywhere outside of them. Together with many and evident disadvantages, there are decided benefits which come from the compulsory military service of some European countries. Let us hope that we may long be spared such a system. Now we do not need it. The benefits which come from the military system are somewhat similar to those which spring from our schools —the sense of order, regularity, promptness, subordination and responsibility. When we consider the possible efficiency of our schools in reference to the teaching of morals, it must come home to us how important it is that the management of our schools shall be free from the taint of dishonesty. It is difficult for teachers to emphasize the necessity of honesty, when the powers over them are giving an example of the opposite quality.

The fourth and last of the things which I have mentioned as essential to success is "a set purpose." Men as I see them vary most neither in their natural abilities, nor in their knowledge, nor in their mental training, though in all these points they vary greatly, but in the matter of definiteness of aim, in clearness and fixedness of purpose. We teachers, give us time, can drive a certain amount of knowledge into almost any person's head, we can give some mental training to almost any pupil. We do not expect the quickest scholar always to be the most successful man, nor do we give up hope of the success of even the dull scholar. A fair acquaintance with the biography of great men would show us that the race is not always to the swift. But the youth without purpose is, I think I may say, the despair of parents, friends and teachers alike. After some consideration of this matter I believe that about the most important of all the requisites is the fixed purpose,—leaving out the third, I am sure it is the most important; for if this be strong it will overcome all obstacles and the other requisites will be secured. I should have more hope of the final success of one who had no knowledge or training, but whose purpose was high and fixed, than of one who had the first two requisites and lacked the last. For the need of the knowledge and training would in time become evident, and he who had the purpose would acquire them.

The fixed purpose, then, I consider of prime importance to the youth who would succeed. and I believe that the school and college years are the time when this purpose is usually established. Indeed, if in all these years nothing else is accomplished, if the youth only discovers what he can do best, or (what amounts to the same thing), what of all things he would like best to do, and determines to do that thing, these years are well and profitably spent. I have always looked on the college course as the time when, by a process of experiment, the choice of a life-work and a dedication to it can and ought to be made. But such a choice comes earlier to some, and to some later or never. Now, what are our educational institutions doing to aid the youth of the land in this momentous decision? What are we doing to lead our pupils to high aims, to inspire them with worthy and great purposes?

I am aware of the many injunctions against ambition, but I still claim that in the good sense of the word, in the meaning which is now commonly accepted, there is no more important work for us teachers than the development in those who come under our charge of worthy and great purposes, aims or ambitions, whichever you may choose to call them. We should try to cultivate in them the spirit of enterprise, the courage to undertake great things, the patience to struggle long for great results, and the faith which will bear them through to success. It seems to me that there is a possibility of improvement in our work in this particular. We may, I think, do more in this direction than we are now doing. Indeed, I go so far as to believe that in times past we have done more than at present. Our reading books once, if I remember correctly, did contain selections which narrated great achievements and dwelt on the doings of great men. Perhaps the reading books of that day were defective in many particulars, but surely in the feature which I am now considering, in the stimulus which they gave to the ambition and purposes of the young, they were better than what we now have. I have looked over a series of these modern readers and the readings which have for several years been required for admission to colleges, without finding a single selection which in any direct and open way gives encouragement to greater or worthier purposes. They may be so chosen as to illustrate in the best manner the many sides of literature as an art, but if they contain any incitement to higher ideals of life or loftier purposes, it is so deeply veiled as to be unrecognizable. In the early days of our Republic the whole people seemed to be saturated with the Lives of Plutarch. Our orators drew their illustrations and our poets their themes from the worthies of Greece and Rome. Patriotism and love of country were viewed as the Romans saw them. The letters in the public press were signed with

Latin names. There was, from this familiarity with Plutarch's writings, a distinct inspiration to higher aims and greater undertakings. But in time the fashion changed. The Greek and Roman heroes were left behind, the Latin signatures disappeared and the great men of our own early history became the theme of our praise. Early biographies of the revolutionary heroes were perhaps more given to panegyric than to searchings for fact. The art of writing biography was, to be sure, but little developed; but the spirit in which these lives were written was right,—it was to emphasize what was great and worthy of imitation and to neglect what was trifling and contrary to the tone and tendency of the whole. I have no doubt that these biographies have inspired many a youth to great life-purposes. And I think they were good works of art. What should we think of a painter who portrayed all the minute imperfections in a portrait, or a sculptor who chiseled in all the wrinkles and blotches? We ought to see these men as they were when they did the great things for which we honor them. Yet this method of writing biography has been supplanted by another which claims to give the real hero, by dissecting him and revealing all the parts in their dire hideousness, and which seems to aim to show how much like ordinary men these great men were. It is something of an indication of the spirit of our times that these anatomical biographies seem to be widely read and enjoyed. I protest that they do not show the men as they were. Errors in perspective are as fatal to a landscape as errors in drawing forms, and any biography which makes prominent the littleness of a great man must approach caricature.

I may bring forward here another subject which has a bearing not only on the set purpose which I am now discussing, but also on the moral standards of which I have spoken. I mean the use of the Bible in our schools.

As to vastly the greater part of this book all men are agreed; as to certain minute parts, they disagree. To spare the scruples of the extremely few, or to avoid discussion and have peace, or because here and there a teacher did not use the book wisely—for some such reasons as these, (for I deny that the majority of any community objects to the use of the Bible because they believe it to be false or its teachings pernicious), for some such reasons as these this book which has established the moral standards of the civilized world and steadily improved them, which is a classic in all European languages, which is quoted in literature more than any other book and is therefore the most essential of all books to an understanding of literature, has been banished from many of our schools. No one can deny that the regular reading from it had a tendency, whether this tendency was strong or not, to establish higher moral standards. And in high ideals of life and service what book has equaled it? And with these high ideals, it gives the encouragement to work and bear with patience that a great end may be accomplished. It holds out hope to him who sees the ideal but hesitates to venture. It is an inspiration to every one whose aims are right.

History and its forerunner, legend, are the great sources from which nations draw their models of heroism and greatness, and of both these we are too young to have any store. I fear our method of teaching the history of the United States does not lend itself to the purpose which we now have in mind. A cursory examination of some of the text-books used does not lead me to expect much help from this quarter. We are then, I fear, reduced to that teaching and influence which come from the good teacher. I need not do more than name Arnold of Rugby and Mark Hopkins to convince you that teachers may give the inspiration of which I am speaking. High minded men, conscious of their great opportunity, controlled by a sense of their high duty, they seemed to give every one who listened to them an impetus toward higher responsibilities and greater achievement. I have no doubt many of us could name men who, perhaps in a smaller measure, have had the same influence on students. I have stated my belief that a fixed purpose is of the highest importance to a student —let me add that I hold the teacher who can and does inspire his students with high aims and resolves, to be the most valuable of his kind. There is no adequate measure of his value.

Such influence as I have asked for is evidently outside of most of our teaching. It comes from the more intimate contact of student and teacher. It is well nigh impossible where teachers deal with large classes in our crowded schools, but is of such extreme value that 1 urge that it be kept in mind.

Whether education does lead to success has always been a question. Whether a general education such as is given by our schools and colleges is necessary or advantageous to those who are preparing themselves for the practice of a profession, whether there is a limit up to which a man ought to study and beyond which he should produce,—such questions as these are most practical and important. To many of them we are not yet able to give a certain answer; the statistics are not extended enough or our experience is not wide enough. Each one must consider all the facts already known, and decide each individual case on its own points.

On the other hand, to other questions the answer is taking definite form. Thus the opinion of the men best qualified to judge is that for those who are to take up the study of medicine, the time spent in preparation for this study in subjects more or less general and liberal is profitably expended; and the strongest of the medical schools are now demanding, or are preparing to demand in the near future, four years of work in some college or scientific school between graduation from a high school and admission to the medical school. This is but a part of the more general movement in the medical profession to raise its standards,—a movement which means much for the well-being of the people and which indicates in unmistakable terms that among the leaders of the medical profession it is believed that general education continued until about the age of twenty-two, and special technical education carried on for four years more, or until the age of twenty-six, conduce to success in the practice of medicine.

In the legal profession a similar movement is going on, although it has not reached as large dimensions as has the movement in the medical profession. In both professions it used to be the custom for young men to study their profession in the offices of practitioners, in other words to serve apprenticeship, and in both professions the recognition is general that the systematic study in the school is more beneficial or more conducive to success than the old apprenticeship system. The standards of admission to the bar are steadily going upward, or in other words, the value of general and special education for the law is more and more generally recognized.

In the ministry I know of no wide-reaching change in regard to a recognition of the value of education. The demand in all the churches has been for more and better educated ministers. If I may judge from the fact that ministers in large cities, and especially in the large and important churches, are as a rule men of college education as well as theological education, there would seem to be a full recognition of the value of wide and liberal education in the ministry. We should not lose sight of the further fact that perhaps nine-tenths of the colleges in the land were founded by ministers of the Gospel primarily to educate men for the ministry.

As to the engineering professions, and other scientific callings, the general consensus of opinion seems to be that a liberal education before undertaking the engineering studies is not on the whole necessary or expedient. Indeed, the scientific schools usually admit students with somewhat less preparation than is required for admission to colleges,—a condition of things which is duplicated in many foreign countries, and for which it is difficult to find any rational grounds. If there is a basis in the nature of men for fixing the age at which the student shall pass from the stricter discipline of the high school to the freer life and more independent choice of studies of the college, as I believe there is, I do not see why the student should go from the high school to the scientific school a year or two years earlier than he would go to the college. The engineering profession, then, while it recognizes the value of education up to the age of twenty-two or three years, has not shown any appreciation of its value beyond that age.

We come here to a very difficult question, one which is just now receiving considerable attention. Does a college education conduce to success in commercial life? Or would the young man who is prepared for admission to college be, on the whole, ultimately more successful in business if he devoted the next four years to liberal study in a college than he would if he went into business life at once? The question is difficult because the terms used are not defined. What is meant by success in the commercial world? Does it mean simply the winning of a fortune in the honest ways of trade? If so, how much of a fortune and in what time? Or does it mean, as it means in the professions, gaining a certain reputation and esteem in the eyes of one's fellows? The rating of a merchant or manufacturer is easy to obtain, but whether his career has been such that we teachers can hold him up to our pupils as an example is a different matter. Are we to take into our computations every man who enters a store or a counting house or a manufactory? They all, doubtless, have an ambition of some kind, and few of them look to remaining all their lives in the lowest grades, through which they must enter, if they enter at all. Then consider the extremely large percentage of those who become proprietors who fail financially. Again consider the specializations of the business world and how difficult it is for a man who has been trained in one branch of business to find openings in another.

I am not inclined to class the work on railroads with the pursuits which are usually called commercial; it seems to me to be comparable to the military service, where promotions depend more on the vacancies above than on a man's ability. In the professions we can with some certainty predict of a young man who has certain qualities that he will, if not gain great wealth, at least win a standing with the others of his profession which is success. I am in doubt whether this is true in business. Again, I do not believe any amount of financial support can give a man a high position in a profession unless he at the same time has first-class ability; while in the business world financial support has the greatest influence. It may not carry a man to the highest position in the business world, but it does lift him out of all the early struggles and give him an immense advantage over those who lack it.

I bring forward all these questions to show how difficult it would be to give a definite answer to the main question if we knew all the facts, of which unfortunately we are almost entirely ignorant.

The statistical method of investigation fails entirely because it is a comparatively recent thing for young men who look forward to a business career to go to college. Probably even now but few young men who intend to go into business go to college except those who have ample financial support—a class which has hardly held its own in the professions. If they succeed in business, their success may perhaps be attributed to their money rather than to their education. However the idea of giving business men a high education is so novel, and the number who have been educated is so small, that any examination into the numbers who have succeeded and failed is simply futile.

Of the four requisites to success which I have named, I have no doubt the third and fourth, "fixed moral principles" and "a set purpose," are as effective in bringing about a worthy success in business life as they are elsewhere. As to the other two, knowledge and mental training, I hold there is no statistical method of determining their value, and, if there were such a method, the facts on which to base a decision are not sufficiently numerous. We have only *a priori* considerations to guide us. If commercial life requires wide knowledge, surely this, like the knowledge required by the lawyer and the physician, can be given more quickly and surely in the educational institution than in the hurry and bustle of practical business life. If commercial life requires trained and quick-acting minds, *probably* the training can be given in the schools and colleges to business men more quickly and surely than it can be gained by experience. This, I hold, is all we can say as to this question now. If successful business men continue to send their sons whom they intend to put into business life to college, perhaps in another generation we shall have facts on which to base a judgment. Meanwhile the educational institutions will probably modify their teaching or enlarge it to conform to what seems to be the best course of study for those who look forward to mercantile pursuits, believing, as did John Knox, that "every scholar is something added to the riches of the commonwealth."

It is one of the difficulties of our profession that our results are so distant. We educate now; the results of our work are not fully evident for a generation. Are we producing men and women who can do the work of the future? Who can tell what the problems of the future will be? We are sure of but one thing, that the future will have its own demands. These, so far as education and training go, we must meet now. Our responsibility is momentous. But when I consider the splendid development of our educational institutions of all kinds and the appreciation of education which seems to increase year by year and day by day, my hope for our future and my faith that the men of that day will be equal to the demands on them is renewed and strengthened.

The Treasurer of the Association, Mr. George N. Carman, of Chicago, submitted his report:

RECEIPTS.

Balance on hand, March 29, 1901..................	$76.39
Fees since March 24, 1901.......................	216.00
Total receipts for the year..................	$292.39

DISBURSEMENTS.

Printing Proceedings of 1901.....................	$105.65
Printing, stationery, and postage.................	10.45
Expenses of Executive Committee.................	19.30
Total expenditures for the year..............	$135.40
Balance on hand, March 28, 1902......................	$156.99

The President then appointed the following committees:

1. To determine the time and place of the next meeting of the Association: President Jos. Swain, Principal E. W. Coy, President J. H. MacCracken.

2. To nominate officers: President A. S. Draper, Superintendent S. O. Hartwell, Principal C. G. Ballou.

3. To audit the Treasurer's report: Principal F. L. Bliss, Professor C. E. St. John, President C. L. Mees.

The subject announced for discussion at the morning session was "Small High Schools in Large Cities."

PRESIDENT CHAPLIN:

Too late for us to secure any one in his place, Superintendent Cooley of Chicago informed the Secretary that he not only could not be present but that he had not written a paper. However, I hope that the other gentlemen will be willing to discuss the subject.

I have the pleasure of introducing to you Principal E. W. Coy of the Hughes High School, Cincinnati.

PRINCIPAL COY:

I am placed in a very peculiar position here today in that I have to discuss a paper that has never been written. That requires a kind of genius that I hardly think I possess.

I wrote Superintendent Cooley asking him what line of discussion he would follow, so that I might be prepared to discuss his paper. He replied that he did not know, so I do not know. We are then to have the play of Hamlet with Hamlet in Chicago instead of in Cleveland.

Now I am in favor, I will say at the outset, of large high schools in large cities. It is very true that these terms are somewhat elastic, and it would not be possible for me to define what we mean by large cities or large high schools in such a way that all would agree upon the definition. So I will not attempt to make a definition.

There is one consideration in favor of large high schools in large cities, and that is the one that grows out of the question of expense. This consideration should, I think, be a controlling one. Of course, there will have to be a limit to the number of high schools in any given city. You cannot place a high school at every man's door. It would not be desirable, if you could. The expense of public education has grown to be so great and is so rapidly growing greater year by year, that we ought not to do anything that will increase this expense, unless we are sure that we are going to add greatly to the efficiency of the work. The public high school must rest upon public approval and we must be careful to avoid any policy that will lead to a forfeiture of that approval. I was told the other day by a gentleman who recently visited New York to investigate the schools of that city that it took one million dollars a year to provide for the natural increase of teachers in that city. This annual increase of teachers is equal to about half the entire teaching force of Cleveland or Cincinnati. So you will see at once that there is an immense expense in this matter of public education. And the public are going to demand better service year by year in the public schools, and the only way to get better service is to pay better wages and so increase the expense.

Now, if we are going to establish small high schools scattered around over the large cities, we are going to increase immensely the expense of running the high schools of these cities. Therefore, I think the better way is to have a few large high schools properly situated in these large cities. The expense of the high school is partly in the building, but very largely in the equipment, the laboratories, reference libraries, etc., and if we are going to establish in a city ten or twelve small high schools, we must have ten or twelve separate buildings, we must have ten or twelve laboratories, physical, chemical and biological, with apparatus and reference libraries in each one, costing for each nearly as much as the equipment for a large high school would cost. So for this reason if for no other the proper policy is to have a few large high schools to accommodate the pupils of the large cities.

There is one other thing to be considered. I know it is true that the attendance in the high schools varies greatly in proportion to the ease of access to the school. If a new high school were built here in Cleveland, for instance, some distance from any of the other high school buildings, there would immediately be a large increase in the high school attendance for the city. This is due in part to the expense of getting to school when the school is situated at a distance.

I think that every city ought to have some arrangement at certain hours of the day for carrying pupils to and from these high schools. I do not know whether this has ever been done, but I believe that it is entirely practicable. It would be cheaper for the city to pay something towards the expense of this transportation to large high schools than to attempt to erect and equip many high school buildings in the different parts of the city. So I say for that reason if for no other that the policy ought to be to have a limited number of large high schools, well supported and well equipped with laboratories, reference libraries, etc. The community, I believe, would not stand the expense of equipping ten or twelve small high schools when three or four might be equipped better with less cost. So I say large high schools for large cities.

THE HIGH SCHOOL PROBLEM.

BY PROFESSOR C. M. WOODWARD, OF WASHINGTON UNIVERSITY, ST. LOUIS, MISSOURI.

The problem of city high schools is a very important one for every large city,—it is a vital one for St. Louis today. The people of the city believe in education; they are loyal to the schools; they patronize the public schools;

yet the high school attendance is abnormally small. In justice to the people of the city I wish to make plain some of the reasons for this. This explanation will lead directly up to a definite and very convincing argument in favor of relatively small high schools. In what follows I omit all reference to colored children and colored schools. My argument applies to them with double force, and I shall consider that branch of my subject elsewhere.

The high school attendance in St. Louis is small for three reasons:

1. First because the preparatory course beginning at the age of six, covers "normally" nine years. The first year is devoted to kindergarten training; then follows a prescribed course of study arranged for eight years. A careful comparison of ages with grades shows that during the five years following the kindergarten the majority of the pupils lag behind the prescribed course of study, i. e., they increase in years more rapidly than they mount the grades. During the last three years, in consequence of the withdrawal of the laggards, or a relatively lighter demand, they mount the grades more rapidly than they increase in years. Hence the pupils who go to the high school enter at about the "normal" age of 15; i. e., 15 years and 6 months.

In most cities the district school course, counting from six years, is only eight years long, so that the "normal" age of entering the high school is 14; in point of fact 14½ years. I am convinced that this abnormal length of the preparatory course partly explains the small attendance at the St. Louis High School.

I do not wish to be understood as saying that a year, or a fraction of a year, is wasted either in the kindergarten during the child's seventh year or in the primary and grammar grades during the next eight years. I wish merely to point out the fact that the St. Louis plan has the effect of reducing the high school attendance below what it would be if the preparatory school training occupied less time.

If St. Louis is to be compared with other cities, it would be nearer the truth to add the attendance in the eighth grade to the attendance in the high school. This would double the figures.

2. The second reason which has kept down the high school attendance has been the long distance the great majority of the pupils must travel to reach the one central school. By actual count 64%* of the pupils ride in the street cars back and forth, the distance varying from one to five miles. The cost, personal risk, and time of such street-travel prove a serious obstacle to thousands of pupils.

3. The third reason for the relatively small high school attendance lies in the high school course of study. The Central School is maintained as a literary high and normal school. It has done two definite things, and done them steadily and well, viz: It has prepared young men for higher education in college and technical schools, and it has trained young women to teach in the public schools of the city. Both these things are necessary and both have been accomplished with credit. Of course it is not to be inferred from the above that the school has done nothing else but fit boys for college and girls for teaching. Less formal courses of study in letters, mathematics and science are allowed, but they are formed from the courses named more by subtraction than by addition. The attractive features of domestic science and art for girls, and manual training for boys have never been incorporated into the high school curriculum of St. Louis. Hence many boys who craved the one, and girls who fancied the other, have either attended private schools or withdrawn from school altogether.

---

*1281 out of 2023.

The effect of the second and third causes is seen also in the extraordinary falling off of boys during, or at the end of, the first year of the high school. Evidently pupils start in at the high school with no definite notion of the course of study and no close estimate of the cost and inconvenience of the double daily journey. Going back six years I find from the Principal's report that:

330 boys who entered in 1895 fell off to 81 in 1896.
353 boys who entered in 1896 fell off to 89 in 1897.
348 boys who entered in 1897 fell off to 79 in 1898.
370 boys who entered in 1898 fell off to 97 in 1899.
326 boys who entered in 1899 fell off to 69 in 1900.

The record of the girls is very little better.

These influences extend to the lower grades. When it is seen and settled that a pupil is not to attend the high school, the conclusion is jumped at that it is less important to complete the grammar school course. We all know how apt children and uneducated parents are to regard a given scheme of study as valuable chiefly because it leads up to another scheme which is an object of desire or ambition. When the desire or ambition for the higher course is wanting, the preparation is regarded as wasted. Hence it follows that the inaccessibility of the Central High School has the effect of cutting down the attendance in the higher grammar grades.

Recalling now the three reasons I have given: The unusual length of the preparatory training; the single central school in a city covering sixty-one miles of area; the lack of certain modern attractive features in the course of study:—I am happy to say that the second and third will disappear within two years. We are preparing to build two more high schools, one north and one south. Each will accommodate some 900 pupils, boys and girls, and each will be provided with the best facilities for manual training and domestic science and art. I have with me the floor plans and specifications of the Wm. McKinley High School. I recommend them as the result of wide comparison and careful study.

The length of the preparatory training is under careful consideration on the part of those able to discuss it intelligently and decide it wisely. Since this paper was presented it has been decided to reduce the preparatory course to one year of kindergarten and seven years of primary and grammar work—eight years in all.

I am now prepared to consider the arguments in favor of numerous small high schools in any large city, instead of one or more large central schools. As I use the word "small" it means a school having about 800 pupils.

The first and great reason for numerous and relatively small schools has already been partly given. I maintain that with numerous small high schools the total high school attendance is greatly increased. If this point can be established no other argument will be necessary. What we want is the greatest possible high school attendance. Given a broad and rational curriculum suited to the demands of the vast army of youth in the city between the ages of 14 and 20, then the larger the proportion in our secondary schools the better for all concerned.

Our experience in St. Louis goes far to prove my point. For several years before the present Central High School building was erected there was room for only the three higher classes in the old building, and the "Junior" or first-year class was provided for in four different district buildings in different parts of the city. Immediately the junior class greatly increased in size. Reports show that for several years that class contained 2.85 per cent of the entire school enrollment of the schools. After the present building was finished and all classes were regularly provided for at the Central, the enrollment of the junior class was only 1.35 per cent,—less than half of what it had been. Many causes combine to produce this result, as strong elsewhere as in St. Louis. I shall give several, but shall not attempt to decide upon their relative importance.

1. *Cost of Car Riding.*—Thirteen hundred of the pupils of the high school ride in the street cars back and forth. Ten cents per day for 200 days amounts to $20.00 per year per pupil. Thirteen hundred pupils pay $26,000 per year. In ten years these car fares would pay for a well-equipped district high school for 800 pupils.

2. *Personal Danger.*—Street car accidents are not rare in any city. In St. Louis they are distressingly frequent. It is perfectly natural that a parent should always wish that his darling child might attend a school within easy walking distance, and it is quite possible that the personal risk a child must incur in two daily rides should turn the scale against a high school course.

3. *Time Wasted in Street Cars.*—The time spent on the cars and in waiting for cars is a waste for which there is no compensation. Half the Central High School pupils spend an hour or two in the unwholesome atmosphere of street cars instead of taking a short brisk walk in the open air. District high schools can be located at local centers, so as to be within easy walking distance of nine-tenths of their pupils.

4. *The Sense of Proprietorship.*—On the other hand the sense of proprietorship which a neighborhood feels for its own high school enhances its value in the eyes of children and parents. They take pride in its architecture, in its teachers, its appointments, and in the advantages it offers. They champion it, they patronize it. This stimulates the attendance, encourages the completion of the course, and enhances the value of the contributory grammar schools.

5. *A Unit School.*—There is in the construction of great power plants a certain balanced group of parts

which the makers call a "unit," and they stand ready to furnish so many "units." It is the same in the organization of a high school. There is an economical limit to the size of a school which may be called "small." It should be large enough to fully utilize an individual set of appliances, but not large enough to require their duplication. For instance, a single botanical laboratory and a single teacher would suffice for a school of 800 pupils. The same is true for zoology, chemistry, physics, and physiology. The same is true for a work shop, a cooking room, a drafting room, an art room, etc. A school of 800 boys and girls makes a convenient "unit." A school of 1200 would require that all such laboratories and shops be duplicated and left only partly used. The "unit" is smaller in the case of a manual training high school than in a classical school.

6. *Smaller Schools are Attractive to Pupils.*—In smaller schools a larger per cent of pupils takes part in public exercises, in athletics, in school club-work of a desirable kind. School excursions are better managed and more generally useful. School honors are relatively more numerous. Hence such schools, other things being equal, are more attractive to pupils.

6. *Smaller Schools are Attractive to Teachers.*—Positions for teachers are also more attractive. There are relatively more principals, more heads of specific departments. When there is but one teacher of chemistry, he feels inferior to none. When there are three teachers of chemistry in one school, two of them occupy subordinate positions.

8. *No Divided Responsibility.*—A single man can discipline and supervise carefully not more than 1,000 pupils of high school grade. If the school is larger, he must have an assistant or vice-principal or a superintendent over a part of the school, and at once there is a

divided responsibility, and we all know that both in the school at large and in a department a divided responsibility is an evil.

9. *Adaptability.*—A district high school may take on some peculiar feature due to its peculiar environment. A principal should study his patrons as well as his pupils, and make sure that the education and culture the children receive or acquire touches their home lives and their parents' interests and sympathies in the manner most profitable for both parents and children.

10. *Emulation.*—With numerous district high schools a wholesome and generous emulation may be aroused between them. Reciprocal courtesies may be extended; exhibits may be compared; competitive class examinations may be given; friendly contests of strength and skill in athletic games and field sports may be held; all these if properly conducted contribute to a desirable *esprit de corps,* which reacts favorably upon the schools and neighborhoods. These reasons, while they admit of elaboration, are here stated as briefly as possible, as becomes one who comes in third in a discussion.

Per Contra—In Favor of Large Central Schools.— There are some arguments in favor of large central schools. The buildings and public exercises can be more imposing; their libraries can be larger. In the case of branches of study not in great demand, reasonably large divisions of students can be maintained with economy. This last reason is sufficiently strong to justify, in a central school for example, an opportunity for the study of Greek, for which the demand is very limited in every city and apparently growing smaller every year. I have been told that while Boston has twelve or more city high schools, there is but one where Greek is regularly taught, and that such Greek classes are open to all the high school pupils of Boston.

Doubtless a similar plan will be followed in St. Louis. The existing Central will always be the center for classical study; and while the McKinley and the Yeatman may offer Latin, science, and the modern languages with their manual training, probably they will not offer Greek.

Again, a building and appliances for 1,600 pupils would cost less than two buildings and apppliances for 800 pupils each, and the argument should be allowed whatever it is worth in the comparison.

Reviewing the whole ground and considering public policy and the public good, the arguments in favor of small district high schools appear to be overwhelming.

PRESIDENT A. S. DRAPER:

Whether large cities should have many small high schools or a few large ones is a question that I do not feel myself at all fitted to discuss. The only practical experience that I have had in connection with this subject was in this city, where there is one great, strong, central high school. It is such in name and it is such in fact. I suppose now it has some 2,000 students. Since that was established there have been four or five erected in different parts of the city. It was not expected that they would ever reach the proportion of the Central High School, and they probably never will.

Now I should suppose that the experience in working out the high school problem here is pretty much what it has been and what it will be in other growing cities. They will begin with one large, central school, and utilize it, and enrich it, and give it liberal support from the pride they have in it, up to the point where they find that it can no longer accommodate the growing numbers, and then they will begin to build outside. And these high schools will not be prepared to accommodate more than 800 to 1,000 pupils.

I should therefore suppose that the conclusion which the city naturally works out in its experience is by far the better one. And I guess that the experience will commonly be that the city will have one great central high school, as long as it can in any way accommodate its pupils in that school, and then it will begin to erect smaller schools. And probably this is as near a wise course as any we can work out for ourselves.

PRINCIPAL ARMSTRONG:

It is very apparent that each one of us has in mind a large and a small high school of his own town. Perhaps the question ought to have been phrased in such a way that a school of 800 would not be a large school in one city and a small one in another.

Chicago now has fifteen high schools, a large school of about 1,500 pupils and smaller schools of as few as 200. Having had a little experience in both these kinds of schools I can say that one of the greatest differences in them is that of expense. As I remember the figures, it costs in Chicago about $50.52 per year for each pupil in a large high school, whereas it costs somewhere in the neighborhood of $80.00 per year for each pupil in the smaller schools. The reason for this difference is obvious. It is due to the smallness of the classes in certain subjects in the smaller schools. I find, for instance, that in a school of 200 we have a class in Greek in the last year of only two or three pupils, a class in Virgil of from five to ten pupils.

The practical solution of this problem would be to give in these small high schools instruction only in branches where enough students were enrolled to make an ordinary class and to leave the other branches for the larger school.

I think the suggestion was made by some one in the Association, I cannot recall by whom, that the school course be divided into three parts, a primary school, an intermediate school and a high school, the intermediate school to come between the primary and the high school and to take in possibly the 7th, 8th and 9th grades. I am afraid if such a movement were started it would mean an increase in the number of years that it would take to complete the high school course; but I believe that the intermediate school plan would solve the difficulty best of all.

I believe that Professor Woodward in his argument carried all of us with him so far as the school of from 800 to 1,000 is concerned. I think he has proved his case for the smaller high school. But I want to call your attention to just one point further, which may perhaps be considered in connection with what Professor Woodward has said. I refer to the proper choice of a location. I have in mind an instance which occurred in Muncie, Ind., where the school authorities had a serious problem before them. In a certain part of the city a class of people, mostly foreigners, had settled, who needed the influence of better surroundings. And this is the way in which the school board met the conditions. They located in that wretched quarter the very finest, best equipped school that was in the power of the city to erect. They finished it with all modern appliances and made it an example of neatness and beauty and fitness to its purpose. Well, the effect of it was rather remarkable. At first the scholars came unwashed and untidy as was their custom, but it was not long before they began to partake of the character of the school itself. They came with cleaner hands and faces, they came with better clothes, and very soon there was really a hope for the bettering of the whole district.

It seems to me that often in our large cities we might achieve great results by bringing the high school and all that it stands for into one of these localities, where otherwise good influences will be lacking.

PRINCIPAL BRYAN:

I wish to say just a word with regard to the intermediate schools just suggested. In St. Louis we find the effect of the intermediate school, as also of all branch high schools, is to increase the number of pupils who discontinue their education at an early stage. They seem to feel that this is a stopping place and not the beginning of a course beyond. I have carefully tabulated the results for some years back and find that the number of pupils who drop out at this point is double the per cent of those who drop out the next year following. And I think that is a matter of great importance where it is our desire to encourage the pupils to go on to the end.

PROFESSOR WOODWARD:

The intermediate school has been taken up by the State Association and it has come up here. It is, of course, a very natural suggestion, but I am very much opposed to it and for the reasons pointed out by Principal Bryan, that is, that the pupils will regard the end of the intermediate period as the proper jumping-off place. So it seems to me that the best thing that we can do in a city is to erect two schools of 1,000 each. So far as I can see, the expense incurred per pupil will not be greater for two schools than one, and the two will reach a greater number than one school can reach.

DOCTOR NIGHTINGALE:

It seems to the Board of Education of Chicago that the city has a large number of high schools, because we have fifteen. And yet if we divided the population of the city by fifteen it would give us only one high school for every 120,000 people, and I venture to say that there is not a town or village of 10,000 people in this country that has not a high school. If, therefore, we had thirty instead of fifteen, we should be better equipped to secure the attendance of the children than we now are, and if we had a high school for every three or four large squares in the city, the high schools would be still better attended. Where the pupils have to go from one to two miles and pay the cost of transportation, it becomes very burdensome to the poorer class of people, even to the lower middle class. And while I would not favor high schools in any city, small or large, for the purpose of increasing the expense of education, still I think that the school of 500 is better than one of 1,000 and I do not think that any person in this Association would differ with one who believes that two schools of 1,000 each would bring better results than one of 2,000. I am glad to learn that there is a spirit throughout the country to increase the number of high schools. The day of opposition to them has passed. They have come to stay. A high school education in the near future will be considered of equal importance with the common school education of twenty years ago.

There are perhaps three out of Chicago's fifteen high schools that have from 275 to 350 pupils; there are seven out of the fifteen that have about 1,000 pupils; there are two or three that have about 1,100 pupils; and there is one that has about 1,500 pupils. I think that 1,000 pupils should be the maximum. The demand becomes too great when one principal must look after the interests of more than 1,000 scholars.

But I give credit to the wisdom and sagacity of the authorities of any town or village that establishes a high school, even though there should be but 75 pupils for it.

I may state an incident in my own experience. When I came to Lake View in 1874 to commence the high school work there, there were but eight secondary pupils in attendance. That school was actually conducted for two months with but eight high school scholars. Of course, we gathered quite a large number of primary school pupils together to swell our number. The following September we had fifteen high school pupils, a large class in the eighth grade, and part of the seventh grade pupils. The next year we admitted one more class, which gave us about thirty high school pupils and the eighth grade. In September, 1876, we had a regular high school with sixty pupils. For sixteen years I was principal of that school, and the largest number we have had at any time was 250 pupils. So while I would not particularly favor the small high school in the largest cities, I would favor the establishment of high schools in any village or town, no matter how small might be its attendance in the beginning. It will grow and prosper and be an institution of power in the community in which it exists.

The following persons also took part in the discussion: Professor M. S. Snow of Washington University; Mr. G. A. Locke, of the University of Chicago; Professor C. A. Waldo, of Purdue University; Superintendent N. C. Dougherty, of Peoria, Ill.; President J. R. Kirk, of the Missouri State Normal School; Mr. Chas. E. Albright, of the Central high school, Columbus, Ohio; and Principal R. R. Upton, of Chillicothe, Ohio.

In accordance with the provisions of the report adopted at the meeting of 1901,[2] the President appointed to the Commission on Accredited Schools the following additional high school members for a period of one year:

Principal Coy of Hughes High School, Cincinnati.
Superintendent Hartwell of Kalamazoo, Michigan.
Principal Bliss of Detroit University School.
Principal Lane of Fort Wayne High School, Indiana.

----

[2]Proceedings of the Sixth Annual Meeting, pp. 70, 71.

Principal Sewall of the Girls' Classical School, Indianapolis.

Principal French of Hyde Park High School, Chicago.

President Seerley of Cedar Falls Normal, Iowa.

Principal Smiley of Denver, Colorado.

Inspector Aiton of Minnesota.

Superintendent Soldan of St. Louis, Missouri.

Principal Volland of Grand Rapids, Michigan.

The President also reappointed for one year the following representatives of the colleges:

President E. B. Andrews, of the University of Nebraska.

President G. E. MacLean, of the University of Iowa.

President J. R. Kirk, of the Missouri State Normal.

Director G. N. Carman, of Lewis Institute, Chicago.

The meeting then adjourned to 2.30 p. m.

SECOND SESSION, FRIDAY AFTERNOON.

The President opened the second session at 2:30 p. m.

The Report of the Commission on Accredited Schools was presented by the Chairman of the Commission, Dean Harry Pratt Judson, of the University of Chicago. (See Appendix for full text of the Report.)

It was moved by Dr. Nightingale that the Report be adopted and printed.

The discussion was opened by President Nicholas Murray Butler, of Columbia University.

President Butler said that he was not prepared to discuss the Report in its bearings upon the educational situation as it had shaped itself in the North Central States, but the principles which the Report embodied were so plain that it was possible for him to consider and to emphasize its relation to the general educational movement of the past decade.

It was gratifying to observe that the Commission had not deemed it necessary to begin all over again. They had built upon the work of their predecessors. The present movement had grown out of an intolerable situation at the point of contact between the secondary schools and the institutions of higher education, and the resulting unrest had first found definite expression in the paper presented by President J. H. Baker, before the National Educational Association in 1891, on the subject of uniformity in school programmes and in requirements for admission to college.

The outcome of this paper was the appointment of the Committee of Ten. The first act of the Committee of Ten was to make use of brains and funds. It organized conferences of experts. The experts having called for about fifty per cent more than the secondary schools could accomplish, it was then necessary for the body of trained administrators composing the committee to take the sum total of the reports and to deal with them in terms of educational practicability. But these ninety experts and the Commitee of Ten were unanimous on one point, namely, that if a subject were taught at all it should be taught for pupils who were going to college and for pupils who were not going to college in precisely the same way. This was an emancipation proclamation. It virtually destroyed the term preparatory school. There was no longer any excuse for giving milk-and-water courses to pupils who were not looking forward to a college career.

The secondary school thus became free to do the best it could in its own way, and the college was put in a position to say that it would accept work well done in the schools by any pupil whether he was preparing for college or not. President Butler then sketched briefly the history of the College Entrance Examination Board.

The results of the examination had proved, he thought, the superiority of the Examining Board to the accredited system, for pupils who were recommended by the secondary schools were in many cases unable to pass the examination.

DOCTOR NIGHTINGALE:

We all came here this afternoon not so much to hear and discuss the report of the Commission, as to listen with ears erect to the lucid exposition of the subject by Dr. Butler, as it affects the institutions of the East, which, because of their age and their traditions, are setting, and of right ought to set, an example worthy of consideration and imitation by the newer born schools of the young but puissant West.

I deem it unfortunate that the distinguished representative of Iowa, the Massachusetts of the Mississippi Valley, should have been prevented from occupying the position assigned him, and that it is left to a layman who is resting from his labors, under political necessities, to open this discussion on behalf of the Association. My remarks therefore will be brief and necessarily desultory. A monumental work has been accomplished east of the Alleghenies, and of that work President Butler of Columbia has been the presiding genius, and to his patient yet determined and indefatigable labors we owe largely the promise of national unity upon this great subject which is to bring the secondary schools, especially the public high schools, the colleges of the people, into harmony with the real colleges and universities of the country without jeopardizing the interests of the high schools which must keep close to the people, and without curtailing the work or lowering one iota the standards and ideals of the universities. All great growths are gradual. It took the last half of the nineteenth century to establish the permanency of public high schools. More than ten years ago the first national movement was started to render these schools efficient instruments in a preparation for higher education. There were storm centers in various parts of the country. The agitation has been persistent There have been concessions, compromises and conciliations. Sufficient objections have been raised by conservatives whom Providence wisely places in the arena of every debate, to prevent undue and hasty legislation. We are approaching the beginning of the end. When this North Central Association, covering this vast dominion of the richest and most progressive states of the Union, and representing more than one-third of its entire population, shall have fallen into line by seconding and adopting the spirit of what the New England and Middle States have done, we shall have linked the free public school system of the nation with the colleges and universities and made possible for our young people an education adapted to individual needs which shall lead them at once into the activities of life or into the halls of our universities where the fittest and strongest may obtain a higher education still.

The report of this Commission which you established a year ago and made permanent is eminently conservative. Those who are most radical in their demands for unlimited elasticity in programmes of study as well as those who still worship the fetich of the fifteenth century can safely unite in their endorsement of this report. It is perfectly safe, there is nothing unique or novel, or, I may say, original in it. It is the result of endless discussion, deliberation and correspondence. Every body of experts who have been making definitions, preparing units of study, and arranging courses in detail, has been consulted and the fruits of their labors are garnered into the storehouse of this Commission.

The herculean task of the Committee of Ten, the recommendations of the Commitee of Thirteen, the results of the Committee of the American Philological Association, of the Modern Language Association, of the American Historical Association, of the Science Department of the National Educational Association, of the Mathematical Association, as well as and especially the exhaustive conclusions of the Examining Board of the Middle States and Maryland, have been incorporated in this report. It only remains for us to adopt it in its entirety, put it into practical operation, amend, modify and enlarge it as circumstances require, and then when the time is fully ripe to appoint or secure a Commission composed of representatives of the New England Association, that of the Middle States and Maryland and of the North Central and Southern States, to formulate a report that shall have force and efficacy throughout the length and breadth of the nation. I can conceive of but one point of difference, and upon this we can agree to disagree, and with no fatal effect upon the national idea. In the East it may be considered necessary to subject candidates to an examination to test their powers of attainment and their ability for advancement. In the Central and far West, the plan, which has met with increasing and gratifying success, will still be insisted upon, that colleges must accept closely guarded certificates from carefully inspected schools. This Association and all associations of colleges and secondary schools will demonstrate their right to permanent existence only when they shall bring into perfect harmony of thought and purpose, those schools which end where the colleges begin. The present is full of promise: great advancement has been made. "Nulla vestigia retrorsum" should be our motto, even though we rise, "ad astra, per aspera."

High schools are multiplying, they are growing stronger, public opinion is being crystallized in their favor, and sometime during this century the better class of them will relieve the colleges of much of the work now done in the first two years and make them in fact, as many are now only in name, true universities.

This report should be adopted, we cannot afford to postpone. If there are radical differences of opinion among us let us settle them today. We are not pioneers in this work. We constitute the rear guard, and there is even now a great gap between us and those next in advance. Let us be willing to follow where others have blazed the way and planted the great hives of educational industry, and educational individualism. Perfection is unattainable. There will always be problems to solve, tasks to accomplish, plans to formulate. What we consider radical today will be conservative tomorrow, and what is conservative today the wildest educational schemer did not dream of a decade ago. The best work this Association ever did was the establishment of this Commission. Its members have been faithful servants, they have labored with no hope of reward but your approval. Grant them this by the adoption of this report and bid them go on with an altruistic spirit until there shall be in the United States a unified system of educational requirements and educational equivalents that shall give to every honest boy and every ambitious girl an opportunity to secure all the intellectual and moral power, along the lines of his natural endowments and his acquired ability, that is possible under the laws of mental reciprocity.

PRESIDENT J. H. BAKER, of the University of Colorado, said that he believed in the Report and hoped that it would be adopted. He was convinced that it was the only basis upon which the North Central institutions could secure unifermity of action. He was interested in the Examining Board and its workings as described by President Butler, but even if it were desirable for this part of the country the plan could not be adopted at present. It was an undertaking of too great magnitude. He hoped that the plan devised by the Commission would be accepted by the Association and put into immediate operation.

PRESIDENT R. D. HARLAN, of Lake Forest University, was of the opinion that the Report was a step in the direction of the examination system. Being a graduate of an Eastern college he had a natural preference for some kind of examination. He hoped that before long the Association might take the further step suggested by President Butler.

PRESIDENT A. S. DRAPER, of the University of Illinois, expressed his regret that President Butler had gone over to the enemy. The teachers of the West had come to look upon President Butler as the upholder in the East of the accredited system. They would be surprised and pained to learn of his defection. Continuing the discussion President Draper said that if the Report of the Commission was adopted he did not clearly see what was to become of the certificate system, as it was already established in most of the North Central States. The university of Illinois, for example, already employed an inspector to travel about the state, inspect the high schools, ascertain what their courses of work were, how many teachers they employed, and how they were equipped for preparing students to enter the university. He wanted to know whether it was proposed to utilize the work of these inspectors without relieving the state of some of the expense. President Draper also commented on the desire for uniformity which found expression in the Report. He was a little skeptical, he said, about uniformity. There might easily be too much of it. He thought this point ought to be carefully guarded.

Later in the discussion President Draper called attention to a provision in the report that no school should be placed upon the list of schools of highest rank to be approved by the Commission, which had not a staff of at least five teachers. He objected to any specification of the number of teachers on the ground that many high schools with only two or three teachers were able to do excellent preparatory work. To such schools a discrimination based solely on the number of teachers would manifestly be unjust.

PROFESSOR A. S. WHITNEY, of the University of Michigan, explained that the list referred to was a list of schools of the first rank about whose standing there could not be any doubt in the minds of the authorities of any university represented in the Association. It was a common list upon which all could agree. But there was no restraint upon the action of individual universities. Each institution could make up its own private list to suit itself.

PRESIDENT J. R. KIRK moved to amend the clause so that the list would include all high schools having ample equipment. The motion was lost.

DIRECTOR G. N. CARMAN then moved that the clause specifying the number of teachers be stricken out. The motion was carried unanimously.

PRESIDENT DRAPER moved the following resolution: That the adoption of the Report shall not be deemed to bind any universities that have already set up systems of inspection of their own, or to change the status of such universities.

The resolution was adopted by consent.

Among those who took part in the further discussion of the Report were the following: Superintendent N. C. Dougherty, of Peoria, Illinois; Principal T. H. Johnston, of Cleveland; President J. H. Barrows, of Oberlin College; Professor H. C. King, of Oberlin College; Principal E. W. Coy, of Cincinnati; Principal J. E. Armstrong, of Chicago; President W. H. Black, of Missouri Valley College; Principal E. L. Harris, of Cleveland; Superintendent S. O. Hartwell, of Kalamazoo.

At the close of the discussion the motion made by Dr. Nightingale that the Report be adopted and printed, was carried unanimously.

It was moved by Professor Denney that the delegates to the Joint Committee on Entrance Requirements in English previously appointed by the Association be continued for two years. This motion was carried, as also a motion by Dr. Nightingale that alternative delegates be appointed by the President.[1]

The meeting then adjourned.

---

[1] The delegates thus continued are Professor F. N. Scott, of the University of Michigan, and Principal C. W. French, of the Hyde Park High School, Chicago. The following were appointed as alternates: Professor M. W. Sampson, of the University of Indiana, and Principal W. J. S. Bryan, of the St. Louis High School.

THIRD SESSION, FRIDAY EVENING.

At the Friday evening session, held in the auditorium of the Chamber of Commerce, the Association was addressed by President Nicholas Murray Butler, of Columbia University, upon the topic, "The College Problem in the United States." The address was delivered extemporaneously, and no report of it was made. The following extract, however, from President Butler's Annual Report to the Trustees of Columbia University, contains so many of the ideas embodied in the address that it will in some measure serve as a substitute:

The whole tendency of our present educational system is to postpone unduly the period of self-support, and I feel certain that public opinion will not long sustain a scheme of formal training which in its completeness includes a kindergarten course of two or three years, an elementary school course of eight years, a secondary school course of four years, a college course of four years, and a professional or technical school course of three or four years, followed by a period of apprenticeship on small wages or on no wages at all.

Four years is, in my opinion, too long a time to devote to the college course as now constituted, especially for students who are to remain in university residence as technical or professional students. President Patton of Princeton University voiced the sentiments of many of the most experienced observers of educational tendencies when he said that: "In some way that delightful period of comradeship, amusement, desultory reading, and choice of incongruous courses of what we are pleased to call study, which is characteristic of so many undergraduates, must be shortened in order that more time may be given to the strenuous life of professional equipment." For quite twenty years President Eliot has advocated this view and in arguments which have seemed to me unanswerable, under the conditions existing at Harvard, has urged that the degree of bachelor of arts be given by Harvard College after three years of residence. At Columbia, and elsewhere, the practice of counting a year of professional study as a substitute for the fourth or Senior year of the college course has in effect established a three-years' college course for intending professional and technical students. The degree has been withheld until a year of professional study has been completed, in deference to tradition rather than from sound educational principle. In this way new conditions have been met without the appearance of shortening the college course. While the policy hitherto pursued in this regard was justified as a beginning toward a readjustment of the relations between the college and the professional and technical schools, it is hardly to be upheld as a final solution of the problems presented. From my point of view it is open to criticism in that it (1) shortens the college course without appearing to do so, (2) divides the interest of the student in a way that is satisfactory neither to the college nor to the faculties of the professional schools, and (3) fails to give the full support to a college course of purely liberal study which is so much to be desired.

There remains a third line of action, namely, that of basing admission to the professional and technical schools of the university upon a shortened course in Columbia College or its equivalent elsewhere. This I believe to be the wisest plan for Columbia University to adopt, as well as the one whose general adoption would result in the greatest public advantage.

One consideration of vital importance appears to have

been overlooked in the numerous discussions of this whole matter, and that is the fact that there is no valid reason why the college course should be of one uniform length for all classes of students. The unnecessary assumption of the contrary view has greatly complicated the entire question, both in the public and in the academic mind. It must be remembered that for the intending student of law, medicine, or applied science who goes to college, three or four additional years of university residence and study are in prospect after the bachelor's degree has been obtained. For the college student who looks forward to a business career, on the other hand, academic residence closes with graduation from college. For the latter class, therefore, the college course may well be longer than for the former. While two, or three, years of purely college life and study may be ample for the man who proposes to remain in the university as a professional or as a technical student, three, or even four, years may be desirable for him who at college graduation leaves the university, its atmosphere, its opportunities, and its influence, forever.

It must be remembered, too, that the four years' college course is merely a matter of convention, and that there are many exceptions to the rule. The Harvard College course was at one time but three years in length, and the collegiate course at the Johns Hopkins University has been three years in length from its establishment. The normal period of residence for an undergraduate at both the English and the Scottish universities is three years. President Wayland, of Brown University, who was in so many ways a true prophet of educational advance, devised a plan for a normal three-years' college course over half a century ago. The question is not so much one of the time spent upon a college course as it is one of the quality of the work done and the soundness of the mental and moral training given. The peculiar service which the college exists to perform may be done in one case in two years, in another in three, in another in four, and in still another not at all.

Since 1860 the changes in American educational conditions have been revolutionary, and as one result the content of the A. B. degree has been wholly altered and that degree has been elevated, at Columbia College at least, to a point almost exactly two years in advance of that at which it then was. In other words, despite the fact that college admission requirements have been raised and much of the instruction once given in college is now given in the secondary schools, particularly the public high schools, the bachelor's degree has been held steadily at a point four years distant from college entrance, with the result that the average age of college students at graduation has greatly increased. Since 1880 the average age of the students entering Columbia College has increased exactly one year, and while no adequate statistics for 1860 are available, it appears to be true that the average age of admission in 1880 was one full year higher than in 1860. The Registrar has made a careful examination of the official records, and reports that in Columbia College we are demanding two years more of time and work for the degree of bachelor of arts than was required in 1860, and one year more of time and work than was required in 1880. President Hyde of Bowdoin College has recently said that "Nearly all the distinguished alumni of Bowdoin College graduated at about the present average age of entrance, and were well launched on their professional careers at about the age at which our students now graduate." He cited the cases of Jacob Abbott and William Pitt Fessenden, who were graduated before they were seventeen; Longfellow, who was graduated at eighteen; Franklin Pierce, John A. Andrew, Fordyce Barker, and Egbert Smyth at nineteen; and William P. Frye and Melville W. Fuller at twenty. Instances might readily be multiplied from the records of the American colleges.

The recent statistics compiled by Dean Wright of the Academical department of Yale University, which show the average age of graduation of the members of the class of 1863 at Yale to have been 22 years, 10 months, and 17 days and that of the members of the class of 1902 to have been 22 years, 10 months, and 20 days, point to what appears to be a striking exception, not yet explained, to the general rule.

So long as there were no graduate schools, and therefore no genuine universities, in the United States, and when the bachelor's degree was the highest academic distinction to be gained in residence, it was sound academic and public policy to make the requirements for the degree of bachelor of arts as high as possible. It was the only mark of scholarship that the colleges could give. As a result, the average age at graduation increased. Now, however, conditions have entirely changed. Nearly, or quite, one-half of the work formerly done in college for the degree of bachelor of arts, is now done in the rapidly increasing number of secondary schools, particularly public high schools, and no small part of it is required for admission to college. This does not appear if the comparison be restricted to admission requirements in Greek, Latin, and mathematics; but it is clearly evident when the present admission requirements in English history, the modern European languages, and the natural sciences are taken into account. The standard of scholarship in this country is no longer set by the undergraduate courses in the colleges or by the time devoted to them, but by the post-graduate instruction in the universities and by the requirements demanded for the degree of doctor of philosophy.

These being the undisputed facts, it would appear to be wise, and possible, to treat the length of the college course and the requirements, both in time and in accomplishment, for the degree of bachelor of arts from the

standpoint of present-day needs and the largest social service.

In my opinion it is already too late to meet the situation by shortening the college course for all students to
three years, although such action would be a decided step
forward so far as the interests of intending professional
and technical students are concerned. When President Eliot first proposed a three-years' course for Harvard
College, the suggestion was, I think, a wise one. But in
the interval conditions have changed again. If we at
Columbia should be willing to go no farther than to reduce the length of the college course from four years to
three, we should (1) find it impracticable both on financial
and on educational grounds to require that course as pre-
requisite for admission to the Schools of Applied Science,
and, possibly, to the School of Medicine, and (2) we
should be unable to resist the pressure for further recon-
struction and re-arrangement that would be upon us before our work was completed and in operation. My own
belief is that Columbia University will perform the greatest public service if it establishes two courses in Columbia
College, one of two years and one of four years,—the
former to be included in the latter,—and if it requires the
satisfactory completion of the shorter course, or its equivalent elsewhere, for admission to the professional and
technical schools of the university. By taking this step
we should retain the college with its two years of liberal
studies as an integral element in our system, shorten by
two years the combined periods of secondary school, college, and professional school instruction, and yet enforce
a standard of admission to our professional schools which,
both in quantity and in quality, is on a plane as high as
the Columbia degree of bachelor of arts of 1860, which
was recognized as conforming to a very useful standard
of excellence. At the same time we should retain the four-
years' course with all its manifest advantages and oppor-

5

tunities for those who look forward to a scholarly career, and for as many of those who intend to enter upon some active business after graduation as can be induced to follow it.

Under such a plan we should have in Columbia College four different classes of students: (1) those who were taking the shorter course of two years in preparation for a technical and professional course, and who would therefore look forward to a total university residence of five or six years; (2) those who were taking the shorter course of two years but without any thought of subsequent professional or technical study; (3) those who felt able to give the time necessary to take the longer course of four years before entering a professional or technical school; and (4) those who, as now, take the four years' college course without any intention of technical or professional study. The second class of students would be a new and highly desirable class, and would be, for the most part, made up of earnest young men seeking a wider and more thorough scholarly training than the secondary school can offer, but unable to devote four years to that end. The third class of students would be able, by a proper selection of studies in the later years of their college course, either to enter a professional school with advanced standing or to anticipate some of the preliminary professional studies and devote the time so gained to more intensive professional work. Undoubtedly many students who now take a four years' undergraduate course with no professional or technical end in view would take the shorter course, and that only, but on the other hand numbers of students would come to college for a course of two years who when obliged to choose between a four years' course and none at all are compelled to give up college altogether. The final result of the changes would certainly be to increase the total number of students taking a college course of one length or another.

The Dean of Columbia College is of the opinion that such a shortened course of two years as is contemplated by this suggestion could readily be made to include all of the studies now prescribed at Columbia for candidates for the degree of bachelor of arts. This shortened course would, therefore, take on something of the definitiveness and purpose which in many cases the rapid developments of recent years have removed from undergraduate study; for it goes without saying that no effort would be spared to make such a two years' course as valuable as possible, both for intellectual training and for the development of character. The student would be a gainer, not a loser, by the change.

If Columbia College should offer two courses in the liberal arts and sciences, one of two years and one of four years in length, the second including the first, the question would at once arise as to what degrees or other marks of academic recognition would be conferred upon students who had satisfactorily completed them.

Two answers appear to be possible. First, we may withhold the bachelor's degree until the completion of the longer course, and grant some new designation to those who satisfactorily complete the shorter course. This has been done at the University of Chicago, where graduates of the junior college course of two years are made Associates in Arts. Or we may degrade—as it is called—the bachelor's degree from the artificial position in which the developments of the last forty years have placed it, and confer it upon the graduates of the shorter course of two years, and give the degree of master of arts for the longer course of four years The latter alternative would be my own preference. Such a plan would bring the degree of bachelor of arts two years earlier than now and would place it substantially on a par with the bachelor's degree in France, the *Zeugniss der Reife* in Germany, and the ordinary degree in course as conferred by the English and the Scottish universities. It would also be substantially on a par with the Columbia College degree of 1860.

In this connection it must be remembered that it is not the A. B. degree of today which is so much extolled and so highly esteemed as the mark of a liberal education gained by hard study and severe discipline, but that of one and two generations ago. The A. B. degree of to-day is a very uncertain quantity, and time alone will show whether it means much or little.

The degree of master of arts is an entirely appropriate reward for the completion of a college course, under the new conditions proposed, four years in length. This degree has been put to many varied uses and has no generally accepted significance. In Scotland it is given in place of the degree of bachelor of arts at the close of three very short years of undergraduate study. In England it signifies that the holder is a bachelor of arts, that he has lived for a certain minimum number of terms after obtaining the bachelor's degree, and that he has paid certain fees. In Germany it is usually included in the degree of doctor of philosophy. In the United States the degree is more often than not a purely honorary designation; although in recent years the stronger universities have guarded it strictly and now grant it for a minimum period of graduate study for one year in residence. At the meeting of the Association of American Universities in February last there was a very interesting discussion on the subject of this degree, and the divergence of policy in regard to it was made plainly evident As an intermediate degree between those of bachelor of arts and doctor of philosophy, that of master of arts has been and is very useful at Columbia. It marks the close of a period of serious resident graduate study, and is an appropriate reward for the work of those university students who have neither the inclination nor the peculiar abilities and temperament to fit themselves for successful examination for the degree of doctor of philosophy. At the same time it must be admitted that the rapid development of the elective system and the widely different standards of the scores of colleges from which our graduate students come, have almost wiped out the distinction between the Senior year in Columbia College and the first year of graduate study. To the best of my knowledge and belief, the fixing of the degree of master of arts at the close of a four-years' under-graduate course would involve no real alteration in the standard required on the part of those coming to Columbia from other institutions. For students of Columbia College it would bring the degree within reach after four years of residence instead of five.

In the case of candidates for the degree of doctor of philosophy, the completion of the longer college course, or its equivalent elsewhere, would of course be required, and also the same minimum period of post-graduate resident study as now. There would be no alteration in the time necessary or the standard now set for that degree, which as conferred at Columbia is recognized as conforming to the highest and best standards.

With the courses in applied science and in medicine fixed at four years, to base them upon a two years' college course would be to elevate them to a proper university standard and to ensure the best possible class of students. The Law School and the professional courses in Teachers College could easily be put upon the same basis.

Reflection and a careful study of the facts will make it apparent that these suggestions are less radical than seems to be the case on first sight. They at least offer a solution to a generally recognized problem, one which has often been pointed to but toward the solution of which little progress has been made. I shall seek an early opportunity of bringing them before the University Council and the several Faculties for full consideration and discussion.

Should Columbia University adopt such a policy as has been outlined, and should the same or a similar policy commend itself to the governing bodies of any other American universities whose problems are similar to ours, a development already in progress throughout the country would be hastened. As the public high schools multiply and strengthen they will tend more and more to give the instruction now offered in the first year, or first two years of the college course. In so far they will become local colleges, but without the characteristic or the attractiveness of student residence. Furthermore, the time would sooner come when colleges, excellent in ideals and rich in teaching power but without the resources necessary to carry on a four years' course of instruction satisfactorily, will raise the requirements for admission to a proper point and then concentrate all their strength upon a thoroughly sound course of two years leading to the bachelor's degree. More depends upon the strict enforcement of proper standards of admission to college than is generally believed; that is at present the weakest point in college administration. The general standard of college education in the United States would be strengthened more if the weaker colleges would fix and rigidly enforce proper entrance requirements and concentrate all their money and energies upon two years of thorough college work than if they continue to spread a college course over four years with admission secured on nominal terms or on none at all.

The policy outlined would, I think, largely increase the number of students seeking a college education, and many who might enter one of the stronger colleges for the two years' course would remain for four years.. The loss of income due to the dropping out of students after two years of residence would be more than made good very soon by the large increase in college attendance.

As the system of higher education in the United

States has developed it has become apparent that we have substituted three institutions—secondary school, college, and university—for the two—secondary school and university—which exist in France and Germany. The work done in the United States by the best colleges is done in France and Germany one-half by the secondary school and one-half by the university. The training given in Europe differs in many ways from that given here, but from an administrative point of view the comparison just made is substantially correct. The college, as we have it, is peculiar to our own national system of education, and is perhaps its strongest, as it certainly is its most characteristic, feature. It breaks the sharp transition which is so noticeable in Europe between the close surveillance and prescribed order of the secondary school and the absolute freedom of the university. Its course of liberal study comes just at the time in the student's life to do him most good, to open and inform his intelligence and to refine and strengthen his character. Its student life, social opportunities, and athletic sports are all additional elements of usefulness and of strength. It has endeared itself to three or four generations of the flower of our American youth and it is more useful today than at any earlier time.

For all of these reasons I am anxious to have it preserved as part of our educational system and so adjusted to the social and educational conditions which surround us that a college training may be an essential part of the higher education of an American whether he is destined to a professional career or to a business occupation. It seems to me clear that if the college is not so adjusted it will, despite its recent rapid growth, lose its prestige and place of honor in our American life, and that it may eventually disappear entirely, to the great damage of our whole educational system.

At the conclusion of the address the following resolution, prepared by President A. S. Draper, was adopted by unanimous vote of the Association:

RESOLVED: That the Association expresses to President Butler of Columbia University deep appreciation of that generous and enthusiastic spirit which has led him so frequently to make liberal gifts of his learning to the educational work of the west, and particularly thanks him for the illuminating and convincing address before the Association at this meeting.   The members of the Association also take the occasion to express their gratification upon his call to the presidency of Columbia University and would gladly have their congratulations upon securing so gifted an executive conveyed to the University and made known at the approaching inauguration.

The Association then adjourned to the library of the Chamber of Commerce, where there was an informal reception to President Butler and the officers and members of the Association.

FOURTH SESSION, SATURDAY MORNING.

The Association was called to order at 9:30 a. m. **by** President Chaplin.

. The session was opened by the reading of papers.

SHALL THE STATE RESTRICT THE USE OF THE TERMS "COLLEGE" AND "UNIVERSITY?"

BY PRESIDENT A. S. DRAPER OF THE UNIVERSITY OF ILLINOIS.

There is no other one word which goes so far to indicate the history and to express the purposes of a free state as the word education. There may be a wide difference between a nation and a state. One may grow naturally enough out of barbarian life without intellectual or moral self-activity, but the other must be created through the affirmative action of the people, by the deliberate grant of the common power, through conventions marked by intelligence and moving in the light of world-progress. A state is the product of a very considerable intellectual and moral advance: its purpose is not mere security from peril, but the assurance of the just rights and the free opportunities of each individual and of the healthful onward march of the whole mass.

Then, on the face of things, it would seem obvious enough that a state may do even more; that it is bound to do anything which it thinks will promote the purposes for which it exists. In all bodies of people there are some who have to be controlled, restrained, and punished.

Standards must differ widely in different peoples. Where the ideals are the highest the policies must be the most aggressive. It seems difficult to say why a state which . exists for moral right and for mental progress is not bound to stop any wrongful or inconsiderate action which deceives its people and thwarts its purposes, quite as much as a tribe or a nation which exists for security alone is bound to stop crimes against person and property.

Colleges and universities are the instruments of free states. They are complicated and costly instruments. Their faculties are constituted of specialists of liberal training and large experience; their equipments are extensive and expensive; their history, their traditions, and the work of their graduates give them character and renown. They are ordinarily continuing and permanent institutions. Their commendations are of recognized value. The very name "college" or "university" conveys meanings which are significant of importance and well understood among intelligent people. And this is the very reason why they have been so much employed by miscellaneous institutions which exist for commercial gain alone. The question is whether such unwarranted use should be prohibited.

Probably this question could not arise in governments which are strongly centralized, for no one would think of employing these names except by the express approval and leave of those governments. Is the free appropriation of sacred things to commercial pursuits one of the privileges which specially inheres in a democracy?

So far as I know there has been but one attempt by an American legislature to limit the use of the terms "college" or "university." That attempt is therefore noteworthy. In the State of New York the legislature of 1892 passed a new university law, and carefully tucked away in the inner recesses of a statute drafted by Melvil Dewey,—an educational artist who never hesitated at an undertaking because its character was unique or its propositions were heroic,—was this rather drastic and aggressive section:

"33. *Prohibitions.* No individual, association or corporation not holding university or college degree-conferring powers by special charter from the legislature of this state or from the regents, shall confer any degrees, nor after January 1, 1893, shall transact business under, or in any way assume the name university or college, till it shall have received from the regents under their seal written permission to use such name, and no such permission shall be granted by the regents, except on favorable report after personal inspection of the institution by an officer of the university. No person shall buy, sell or fraudulently or illegally make or alter, give, issue or obtain any diploma, certificate, or other instrument purporting to confer any literary, scientific, professional or other degree, or to constitute any license, or to certify to the completion in whole or in part of any course of study in any university, college, academy or other educational institution. Nor shall any person with intent to deceive, falsely represent himself to have received any such degree or credential. Counterfeiting or falsely or without authority making or altering in a material respect any such credential issued under seal shall be a felony, and any other violation of this section shall be a misdemeanor; and any person who aids or abets another, or advertises or offers himself to violate the provisions of this section, shall be liable to the same penalties."

Although apparently there has been no other attempt to restrict the use of the terms "college" and "university" there has been much discussion and some little progress towards the state control of institutions which assume to confer scholastic degrees. In several other states there have been movements against the conferring of degrees except under the authorization of the state, and attempts to fix the minimum limit of endowment, faculty, entrance requirements and course of study, precedent to the grant of authority. But it must be said that legislation in this direction has not so far met with ready or general favor. It has been opposed by interests which either feared its effect upon themselves or misapprehended its purpose and were able to make legislators conclude too quickly that it was aristocratic in its tendency and a needless limitation upon democratic freedom.

As between the two propositions that the degree conferring power must come from and be regulated by the state, and that the use of terms by which institutions are designated may be restricted by the state there is probably no difference in principle, and if they are to be enacted into law elsewhere they may very well go together as they do in the New York statute.

As I understand it, this kind of legislation is intended to remedy two evils which have resulted from our growth in population and in wealth and are the offspring of the educational advance and of rampant commercialism. One is the naked fraud, but poorly disguised, of selling spurious degrees for cash; the other deludes the young or the inexperienced by pretending to do what it is incapable of doing. Men who are responsible for the first are moral criminals, and statutes should make them legal criminals and punish them for it. The degrees of culpability for the second are endless, and the shades of responsibility are infinite. Men sometimes deceive themselves. Some do not know, and some do not care. Some mean well and do ill. They do not see the line between genuineness and pretence, between the real and the spurious. It is said that this misleads the crowd; that it discredits the worthy; that society must protect its members and promote the common welfare by determining by whom and how works of *public* interest shall be carried on, and by limiting terms of well settled interpretation to the use intended by the very common sentiment.

There are concerns, some of them incorporated under the forms of law, which have no building, no campus, and no teaching staff, and yet which are assuming to confer literary, scientific, and professional degrees for cash; and their transactions are not few in number. They need not take our time; there is no room for a question about them, for the fraudulent intent is clear, and society is bound to outlaw and to punish educational as other frauds.

But what should the state do as to institutions with more or less genuineness of purpose, and more or less ignorance, which are pretending the impossible as a means of livelihood? There are institutions advertising themselves as colleges and universities and assuming to confer degrees, which lack the means to do the work that any intelligent community can accept as the foundation for the academic degrees. What about them? There are concerns with signs which are absurd and amusing. Hard by the deep shadow of one of the most prominent universities of the country I saw recently the glaring insignia which proclaimed two institutions of learning within. One taught blacksmiths, and was a "Blacksmithing University," and the other trained barbers, and was a "'Shaving College." What about such as these and others of the same species, but with less unconscious humor about them?

If it is difficult to make the crowd see the wrong which these things work to some and the demoralization which they bring upon the solid educational work of the country, it will not be necessary to urge that phase of the subject here. We turn at once to the discussion of what course should be taken, and ask whether these matters come within the scope of the lawful action of a democratic state, and if so what is expedient in the premises.

We are upon very solid ground when we accept the

definitions of the American and English Cyclopædia of
Law (v. 27, p. 632) as to what colleges and universities
are. It defines a university to be "an institution of higher
learning consisting of an assemblage of colleges united
under one corporate organization and government, afford-
ing instruction in the arts, sciences, and the learned professions and conferring degrees." It declares a college
to be "an organized assembly or collection of persons
established by law and empowered to co-operate for the
performance of some special function, or for the pro-
motion of some given object which may be educational,
political, ecclesiastical, or scientific in its character."

It has been sufficiently held by the American courts
and is generally accepted that a college or university
cannot do things which are not specifically or impliedly
granted in the charter or the act under which it is incorporated, and has no power to confer degrees or to grant
diplomas unless the power is expressly given by the legislature.

This is much, for it goes very definitely to the source
of the degree-conferring power. It might well be made
more of, because it is so much easier to accentuate the
powers of legislatures in the minds of legislators and to
induce them to fix the terms upon which they will grant
the powers of the state than it is to procure the passage of
laws making misdemeanors of conduct which does not
seem very heinous to the legislative mind. And it must
be said that good, strong, affirmative legislation, and
much of it, upon the equipment and powers of colleges
and universities, upon the conditions precedent to the
granting of degrees, would work a very invigorating
effect, both directly and by reflex action, upon the educational situation of the country.

But of course this does not meet the question. What
is to be done with those who want to follow an educational
business for what money there is in it, and who cannot

carry on that business upon a plane to command the approval of the state? What about those whose ignorance, or indifference, or cupidity, leads them to make public pretenses which are impossible and absurd, misleading and demoralizing?

If the state is definitely to assume exclusive authority over the power to confer academic degrees and to prescribe the organization, resources and outfit of colleges and universities, and then to outlaw all concerns which do not meet its requirements, and prohibit them from using the names which it reserves for the institutions which it sanctions it must do more than grant authority to do what it approves; it must stop others from doing, or pretending to do, the same things without its approval. This involves the exercise of what is called the police power.

The police power, its growth, its scope, and its limitations, can only be referred to here. It cannot be discussed, for volumes are inadequate to its comprehensive exploitation. It would be presumptuous even to attempt to define it. The most learned judges and text writers have declared that it cannot be defined. In the most general way it may be said that it is the power which has arisen in organized society to regulate its affairs in the interests of the common welfare and progress. It not only allows; it forbids and punishes. It has enlarged and extended as communities have increased and society has advanced. It goes beyond the punishment of the recognized crimes and concerns itself with the life and health of the citizen, with the enjoyment of private and social life, with the comfort of existence in dense populations, and with the intellectual progress of the mass.

The police power is the trenchant instrument of democracy, and for reasons quite obvious it has had its fullest development and its widest application in this country. The matters upon which it has assumed to act can hardly be enumerated, but the comprehensiveness of its scope may be indicated by a partial statement of them.

It has undertaken to make dwellings sanitary, and to provide means of escape from fire, to regulate the sale of drinks and to prevent the adulteration of foods, to prevent nuisances and to stop games which are hurtful or demoralizing. It supervises transportation companies, insurance companies, building associations, banks, and the like, and sternly prohibits the carrying on of these businesses except by the leave of the state. It regulates innkeepers, hack-drivers, and auctioneers. It forbids the practice of many of the professions until the candidate has passed such tests as it prescribes. It refuses permission to teach in the schools until the preparation which it exacts has been accomplished. It even assumes to interdict many of the occupations of skilled labor until it places the mark of its approval upon the workman, and it controls many of the ordinary vocations for the sake of the common good.

Under this power it has been held that the state may tear down a house which is going to decay or one which promises to be food for a conflagration; that it may slaughter cattle with infectious diseases; that it may compel vaccination and confine the insane or those afflicted with contagious diseases; that it may restrain vagrants and beggars and drunkards; that it may suppress obscene publications and houses of ill fame; that it may establish the places where and the conditions upon which certain legislative callings may be carried on; and that it may fix the price at which water may be sold by one who has a monopoly of it.

The highest court in the land and by far the most august in the world has held that under the police power a state may regulate and fix the charges which the owners of private property holding themselves out to do a general business may exact of customers who require their service and the use of that property whenever it appears that they have a monopoly of the business and it has come to be of public interest. The right to regulate and control involves the right to suppress if conditions make it necessary. The Supreme Court has held that a valuable property built up under the protection of the law may be confiscated and destroyed without compensation under the police power of a state after an amendment to the state constitution had made the business carried on in that property unlawful, and this notwithstanding the provision in the Federal Constitution against taking property without due process of law, and the other one against impairing the obligation of contracts. The gist of all this is that when a public interest is involved the legislature may intervene and go all lengths to promote it; that whenever a matter is determined to be of a public as distinguished from a private character the state may do whatever in its judgment may be necessary concerning it.

In a word it may be said that the police power of the state extends to every matter involving the well being of the community whether it be moral or social, industrial, or intellectual and educational.

There are of course limitations upon the exercise of this power. It must not contravene the principles established in the charters of English liberty, and it must not get in conflict with the provisions of our state and federal constitutions. This gives rise to the most intricate legal questions. No law questions have ever so taxed the learning of any court in the world, and, it may be added, have been so safely met, as those which have required the Supreme Court of the United States to determine whether the exercise of the police power in certain cases was in conflict with provisions of the Federal Constitution, and particularly whether it was obnoxious to the civil rights amendments thereto.

Of course the exercise of the police power must be in good faith, and not to gain any fatuous or sinister end.

6

It cannot be used as an instrument of persecution. One's right to pursue any business he chooses up to the point where it conflicts with the common welfare is fundamental, but everything hurtful to the *public* interests may be restricted and prohibited. Whether a statute invades a fundamental right, whether it helps or hurts the common good, whether it conflicts with any of the provisions of the constitutions are questions for the courts. Therefore the exercise of the police power must rest in the sound discretion of the legislative branch, and must have the approval of the judicial branch of the government. Within these limits it is untrammeled. The courts will uphold the legislative discretion unless it has fallen into fundamental error.

Fortunately in our system the responsibility for public education is with the same authority which is charged with the proper exercise of the police power. Our educational systems are state systems. They are not city, county, town or district systems except as the state legislatures delegate authority to cities, counties, towns or districts. Such delegation of authority may be modified or taken away. The supervision of educational work, the provision and direction of educational instrumentalities, are with the states. These things have never been ceded to the Union. Many of the state constitutions say so. The legislatures and the highest courts in many of the states have said so. The Supreme Court of the United States has said so. The Federal Government may aid and encourage, but it cannot direct or control education in the states. Of course it may and must in the territories. It has never claimed anything else. The Constitution of the United States contains no reference to the matter. That great document is silent upon the subject of first public concern. It is not because the men who framed it were ignorant or indifferent. They were the very best men in the country; half of them were college graduates. It is because it was deemed best to leave the whole matter with the states, and experience has proved, overwhelmingly, the wisdom of the course. The plan is a wise and beneficent one: it has located authority and responsibility within the popular reach: it has given the educational system its largest opportunities, while it has made it adaptable to the circumstances of all sections of the country.

Educationists of all others should understand this, but the very elect get befogged about it. Last summer when the adverse report of its commitee on a national university was presented to the National Council of Education some of the past-masters of American education became frantic over it. Happily Mr. Carnegie's munificence has relieved the whole situation, made further discusssion of a national university superfluous, and released Congress from the temptation to do much shuffling and prevarication to educational constituents and lifted the courts out of peril of differences with the Council of Education.

It is a power which under our system inheres in the several states. It has never been ceded to the general government and has never been claimed by it. It is a sacred trust which the people have confided in the state legislatures, and which those bodies will neither be allowed to abuse nor divest themselves of, but must administer for the good of all, without fear and without favor.

All this points very conclusively to the undoubted power of the states to do whatever they may think well to uplift and advance education. Nothing which they may do in this connection is likely to impinge upon any of the fundamental rights of man, or to conflict with any of the provisions which the well-being of the common brotherhood and interstate comity have led us to place in the Federal Constitution. There can be no doubt of the right of any of our states to prohibit the conferring of academic degrees without express authorization, and to restrict the use of names to institutions which it approves and for which it reserves them.

It must be said, moreover, that the state has a responsibility and a duty as well as a power in the premises. Colleges and universities are historic. They have come down to us out of the very dim past. By the common understanding and usage of civilization they are creatures of the sovereign power. Academic, scientific, and professional degrees are things of real value, distinctions obtained by long labor under state supervision and certification. They are authoritative commendations to public confidence; often they grant the state's permission to practice professions; the system is not only to commend attainments and certify scholarship, but to save the public from imposition; they are things in which there is a property value. By the common understanding and usage of civilization degrees can be conferred by colleges and universities alone. Therefore no degrees can be conferred except through the leave of the state, and there are no colleges and universities unless set up or authorized by the state. Then all other institutions calling themselves "colleges" and "universities" and all degrees they confer are in a legal and public sense spurious, and it is the business of a state to use the police power to suppress things which are spurious, in order that they may not mislead the ignorant and seem to lessen the true value of things that are real.

If a man holds himself out to the public to carry on public work the law presumes that he has the skill and ability to carry on his calling, and if he has not he is liable in an action of tort to any who employ him and suffer by his lack of skill and ability. Is not the state remiss if it permits one to impose thus on the public, and does it not render itself in a way a party to the fraud and injury?

There has already been much legislation throughout the country against impure and imitation foods. Oleomargarine, or imitation butter, has in places been altogether prohibited. More generally the use of coloring matter, employed to make people think it was butter, has been prohibited. At the present session of Congress a bill has passed the House and seems likely to pass the Senate laying an internal revenue tax of one-fourth of one cent per pound upon oleomargarine when not colored to imitate butter, and a tax of ten cents per pound when any coloring matter enters into it. The laws have very generally required the vendors of oleomargarine to stamp plainly the true character of the contents upon the package. And all this is not in the interests of health, for it is admitted that oleomargarine is not unwholesome, but in the interest of honesty and fair dealing. It is all done to save the public from imposition, and to protect the dairymen against competition in the dark with an imitation which can be produced at a small part of the cost of the real article. Does not the same principle apply to fraudulent colleges or imitation universities?

Of course there are those who take the view that the function of a state is to assure immunity from hurt to person and to property. They seem to think that the only right of a state is to protect its citizens from aggression. That is not the accepted view in this country. The general view is that it is not only the business of the state to protect the lives, liberty, and property of the people, but also to promote the health, peace, order, morals, and learning of the nation. This it is which, in its public manifestation, distinguishes democracy from the more consolidated forms of government. It is at once the mission and the measure of our democracy. Thank heaven our governmental system is a marching and an advancing one. It was never intended to stand still. Principles, the guides of action, are imbedded in conscience and are stable, but moral and intellectual life is to move forward and upward. The combined power of the people is to protect it, guide it, and help it on its way.

It goes without saying that it is the function of the state to encourage moral and intellectual self-activity. It is to help on educational enterprises which are meritorious though young and weak. But this does not mean that the state is to have no educational standards, that it is to permit the indiscriminate exercise of that authority of which it is the exclusive source and which it is bound to use with deliberate and sound discretion, or that it is to allow the misappropriation for commercial or other purposes of terms which have come to be well defined, which imply public service, and which can be rightfully applied only to institutions capable of promoting the national ideals and desirous of serving the general ends.

As society grows in volume and advances intellectually the necessity for a larger use of the common power for the common good becomes more imperative. The whole world is relative. Ideals and policies change with conditions. Rural life does not require the same regulative policies that are needed in urban life, for rural life is happpily free from much of the deceit and imposition so rampant in urban life. Newly settled states do not sustain the same regulative policies in education or other matters which the stability and the strength of older states require them to enforce. The advance of states to real statehood, the rise of democracy in structure and in spirit to the point where it can stand strains and gain confidence, where it can suppress the evil and give free flow to the good there is in the lives and souls of the people, is measured by the common understandings which are so well intrenched that they need not be written in the law books, or else by statutes and decisions which its constituted authorities have made States are not comprised exclusively of people who can live in peace and security and grow in morals and intelligence without any government at all. Government is not a pastime. States must limit and restrict the wrong and set up institutions and point the true way. Learning, the life-blood of democracy, will not flow in the veins of a commonwealth which cannot understand this or is so weak and so lacking in character that it cannot exercise its authority to accomplish these ends.

Then it seems to me that upon the subject under discussion we can come to no other conclusion than that the state should not allow any institution to confer academic degrees except by its express authority, and that it should restrict the use of the terms "college" and "university" to institutions which have the state's authority to confer degrees.

And it would seem also that institutions should not be allowed to appropriate names which belong to all the people. The names of states, or cities, or towns, should not be permitted to be used except by the special leave of the state, or the city, or the town, to which they belong, and perhaps better still they should not be permitted to be applied to institutions other than those which are set up, maintained, and controlled by the state, or city, or town, whose name they would bear. Any other course is misleading, deceives some, and wrongs all, for it gives to a few what is within the proprietary ownership of all.

SHOULD THE USE OF THE TERMS UNIVERSITY, COLLEGE AND SCHOOL BE LIMITED BY LAW?

BY PROFESSOR DUDLEY P. ALLEN, MEDICAL DEPARTMENT, WESTERN RESERVE UNIVERSITY.

The question "Should the Use of the Terms University, College and School be Limited by Law," has been given me by your committee on programme for consideration. I had a short talk with a member of the committee and received from him a note in which he says, "It is better for you to take up the relation of the one to the other and what the state owes to them and they to the state." I shall, therefore, present what I have to say to you along these lines and leave the legal questions, particularly those of a technical sort to my friend, Mr. Hopkins, Dean of the Law School of Western Reserve University.

The subject naturally divides itself under various headings: First, is it desirable for the state to determine the relative standing of universities, colleges and schools? If desirable, in the second place is it practical? Third, if practical, would such a division be legal? In discussing the first proposition, viz., Is such a division of terms desirable? the question cannot be settled wholly along theoretical lines. There are certain practical considerations which are of moment. Of course in thinking of the relations borne in America by the various departments of instruction to each other one naturally compares them with the conditions as they exist in Europe, less perhaps with England than with France and Germany. As you all know Germany has schools first for the instruction of young children; second, those of a more advanced sort, giving instruction in common branches; third the gymnasium, which is a preparatory school, preparing students for study in universities and corresponding in a degree to the college in America, although giving a less extensive, though undoubtedly a more thorough training; and fourth, the university proper which is made up of four faculties, the philosophical faculty, the theological faculty, the law faculty and the medical faculty. No school in Germany would be considered a university without these four faculties. In addition to these there has been established in Germany what is known as the Realschule or Technical School. It would not be in place to discuss in this paper the relative merits of institutions of learning as they exist in Europe and in this country. According to the standards which exist in Europe a university is pre-eminently a school in which only advanced instruction is given. No one is admitted to it until he has a thorough preliminary training. According to these standards there is scarcely a university in the United States. Many schools in the United States are called universities, in which the four faculties do not exist. In some of these so-called universities the instruction is decidedly elementary, being by no means equal to that which is given in many institutions which are called colleges. I think one needs but to call to mind the various institutions of learning with which he is acquainted to find that we have many colleges in which is given a certain amount of real university training and many universities in which little is given beyond college training. On the other hand, it is imperative that we should consider the history of education in the United States and the method of its development, in order to understand what its future probably will be. The one institution which has been the most fixed factor in American education up to the present time is the so-called college. The college originally gave classical training, but as the years have gone by a decided effort has been made toward broadening or diversifying the training, so that in addition to a certain amount of mathematics, Latin, Greek and philosophy there has been added a large amount of instruction in other lines, particularly those relating to science. Many of these colleges are in cities of small size or in villages. Many of them have achieved a great reputation and have large endowments, adequate to the carrying on of the work for which they were originally created. It is wholly improbable that colleges of this character can become universities in the strict sense of the word, since their location and endowments are not of a sort to make it possible. These institutions will, however, continue to exist. The long history behind such colleges as Amherst, Williams, Dartmouth, Bowdoin and, in the West, Oberlin, not to mention others, and the extensive buildings, laboratories, equipment and endowments already in their possession render their future secure. On the other hand, there are colleges which originally were in small cities, but around which have grown up large populations, such as those about Harvard and Yale, and to which great endowments have been given, so that their development is more nearly along that of university lines than other institutions. In addition to these are other institutions of great prominence receiving state aid, as well as institutions which have been established in great centers of population, such as Columbia University, Western Reserve University, Johns Hopkins and the University of Chicago, which tend to grow along the same university lines. Beside these so-called colleges we have scientific schools, as the Institute of Technology in Boston, the Sheffield Scientific School, Clark University of Worcester, and the Case School of Applied Science in Cleveland. One has but to regard the different lines of work carried on in these institutions and understand the absolute lack of correlation between their different departments to see that education in the United States is carried on in an absolutely illogical way, devoid of system and lacking in many of the advantages which would be incident to some established order.

The absence of all order in the conduct of education in America would seem to answer the first question which we have under consideration, viz., Is it desirable that some order be established? It seems to me that the answer to this must be absolutely in the affirmative, and that no man who has any connection with education can but appreciate the great necessity for the establishment of some relationship between the various grades of education. It is a much easier thing, however, to say it is a desirable object to accomplish than to point out the way in which it is to be accomplished. I feel myself out of place in speaking before a body of educators, upon a subject with which you as educators are so constantly occupied. As a teacher of medicine, however, the questions before us have constantly forced themselves upon me on account of the inadequate preparation for medical study presented even by college graduates. It is quite possible that a wider acquaintance with the subject might lead me to other conclusions, but there are certain thoughts in this direction to which I desire to give expression. The thing which I observe is this: in all our cities and villages are common schools and high schools. A child is put in at one end of the course and ground out at the other end in a certain number of years. In many cases, I do not say in all cases, as I have no question there are some notable exceptions, the course of study is not laid out with any definite purpose. A student's course when finished in the high school may terminate his education or it may prepare him to enter college, as we say. If it terminates his education it may perhaps have given him a fair degree of information and mental training. If it is to prepare him to enter college, I believe under most circumstances he is but poorly fitted to do so. Perhaps saying what I do before teachers better qualified than myself to judge of this, I may be considered guilty of unjust criticism and perhaps of rank heresy; but I venture to say that there are comparatively few public schools in the United States which, as a matter of fact, prepare youth for college as well as they are prepared in schools whose special function it is to carry on this sort of work. A wide inquiry among teachers in colleges has led me to this conclusion. In the first place much of the teaching is not of the first rank. In the second place if a student is to have college training subsequent to his high school training, there is no use in wasting his time in elementary instruction in branches in which he will receive thorough instruction later. The great objection to the present method of carrying on work is three-fold, first, much time is lost in needless instruction of the elementary type, second, little opportunity is offered for a student intelligently capable to progress more rapidly than one who is dull, and third, the instruction given along needed lines which prepare a student for college is not sufficiently thorough. The courses of instruction have been suited to the ability of mediocre students and little premium has been put upon the rapid individual development of students more able to progress. As a result all are ground out in a certain number of years and at a given age. This criticism is not only true of common schools but it is true of colleges.

If a boy going to college is to terminate his education with his college course one line of instruction is perhaps desirable. If, on the other hand, he is to enter upon some professional study, there is no use of his wasting his time in the college where the instruction is poor along professional lines if he may be better instructed along these lines later in a professional school. I speak with freedom upon this subject, because I think I am sufficiently acquainted with it to do so, and I say without a moment's hesitation that instruction along so-called scientific lines in most colleges is wholly inadequate to take the place of instruction which is given in the best professional and technical schools. That line of instruction with which I am of course best acquainted is instruction looking toward the study of medicine. and the best medical schools find that men who come to them from the large majority of colleges, seeking advanced standing on account of subjects already studied during college courses, are by no means so well trained as men who are taught in the professional schools themselves. This must necessarily remain so unless colleges are prepared to employ men thoroughly trained in this direction and spend a vastly greater amount in equipment than most of them are doing at the present time. The result of these conditions is that time is lost in preparing boys for college and that time is lost in college in preparing men for professional schools. It necessarily follows that when young men go to professional schools they are from two to three years older than they might reasonably be expected to be. In a word they have lost, when their whole education is considered, probably more than three years over and above what would be necessary if there were proper correlation of instruction between various schools. It seems to me, therefore, that it is beyond all possible question that some understanding of the terms school, college and university is highly desirable, and that there should be some correlation between these various departments of instruction..

I will now turn to the consideration of the second part of the proposition before us, viz., Is such a division practical? In such a complex condition of affairs as exists at the present time it is of course impossible for any man to point out a method which will be wholly satisfactory to all concerned. I do not know that any method could be established which would solve all the difficulties incident to the consideration of the question. I have often sought in my own mind a solution of the problem and the line of thought which has occurred to me is something as follows. In the first place it is the function of the state to give to the bulk of the children of the state the sort of education which will best fit them for citizenship. The majority of children can have but a limited education. It is important, therefore, that this should be of the best sort. It is much more desirable that a small town should give a common school education along the lines most needed for the great body of students, than that it should give a less efficient education to these and attempt to give a preparatory college course to a small number of students who desire further study. I should say, therefore, in the first place that the state might establish a standard of instruction which must be reached in all common and high schools before these schools are permitted to give preparatory training for college and that no funds of a municipality should be taken for the purpose of giving preparatory instruction for college until the very best provision has been made along the lines of common education. If, after common education has been well provided for, a town or state desires to give further preparatory training for college, it may be permitted to do so. I see no reason why the state should not insist upon this. For the state to undertake to regulate the course of study in colleges not supported by the state would be a much more difficult matter. As I have already pointed out in the first part of my paper the college is an institution peculiar to the United States. It does not exist elsewhere. Many of our colleges have behind them a long and honorable history, they have a large body of alumni and are possessed of extensive endowments, buildings and equipment. They are corporate bodies and I question if the state would be able to regulate their courses of instruction. The question is, How can the state bring any efficient influence to bear upon the problem of higher education? It seems to me that this problem must be undertaken by states rather than by the federal government. Obviously, the federal government would scarcely undertake to direct the courses of instruction in venerable institutions such as Harvard,

Yale and Princeton. I question if the older states of the Union would be able to do much in this direction, thoroughly provided as they are with institutions of instruction of the higher sort. It would be a relatively easy matter for states which already have great state universities and few endowed colleges to bring strong influence to bear in this direction. They doubtless will work out this problem in their own way. The question comes up, What is to be done in other states, already provided with a sufficient number of colleges for every purpose of classical instruction and in which either there is no state university or the university, if it exists, has not reached a high degree of development.

It would not be unreasonable that the larger universities and colleges with great endowments, located in prosperous cities, should seek to develop themselves along the line of true university education. On the other hand, is it not possible that as the years go by, the colleges in the smaller towns may come to limit themselves more to a course of instruction preparatory to university work?

There are schools, however, in which any such division would be difficult. At a dinner given me some years ago in Boston, at which I met a large number of instructors in Harvard University, the question came up of the relationship borne by the professional schools of that university to the corporation. I remarked at that time that it seemed to me Harvard University was losing, or had in the past lost, a magnificent opportunity. As a graduate of the medical department of Harvard I had not been made to feel that this department bore any true relationship to the University itself, and I did not believe that the graduates of professional schools had any great share of affection for the University. I also stated that I thought this was a great misfortune for the University, since I believed it possible that all graduates of the professional schools might become enthusiastic supporters of the University itself.   At a Harvard dinner given here some few weeks ago the same problem came up and a gentleman remarked to me that up to the present time the backbone of Harvard University had been its academic department. I do not question that this is true. It is possible that it may always remain so, but it seems to me that if it be true at Harvard. and that she must always retain her academic department, there are few universities in the great cities of the United States that would not be strengthened rather than weakened if they were to elevate their course of instruction to the true university standard and admit no one who had not already received a thorough preliminary training or what we ordinarily call a college course.   On the other hand, instead of the colleges in our smaller towns striving to become universities, would it not be far better for them to content themselves to do thoroughly first-class college work.   Their location and their facilities are such as to enable them to do this to the very best advantage.   Besides I am inclined to think that the best place for the undergraduate is in a college town where he is under a certain amount of restraint and control, and where he has the benefit of the literary atmosphere which belongs to many of these college towns and which is of vast advantage in the culture of a young man.   Even a slight acquaintance with Oxford or Cambridge. to say nothing of some of our own university towns, will, I think, be sufficient to convince any one of the value of environment in the culture of a student.   If some relationship could be established between college and university I believe that our rural colleges would become more efficient and that the training which they give would be more thorough, and I believe also that the universities in our great cities, if relieved of the so-called "college course," would not only receive the cordial support of the vast number of colleges in our small towns but would also become broader and stronger.

In discussing the question further I do not know how I can do so better than to consider the state of affairs which exists in Ohio today. since the conditions are the same in Ohio as in a good many states around us. We have in Ohio between thirty and forty colleges. The last available statistics placed the assets of these colleges at about $16,000 000 Doubtless this figure is much too low. I presume that the total amount would be a vastly greater sum. Some of these colleges have a long and honorable history and give a thoroughly first-class course of undergraduate instruction. There is in the state no completely equipped university. according to the standard given us by the universities of Europe. The state has no control over its colleges and I doubt if it could obtain it constitutionally. What can it do? About thirty years ago, under a grant from the national government. a school of mechanical and agricultural instruction was started by the state at Columbus. This school has increased until it comes before the legislature this year asking a grant of about $400.000, and it also asks that this grant be made perpetual. It has from the United States government about $25.000 and as interest on funds given it by the general government it receives about $33,000. These latter sums, together with moneys received from laboratory fees. etc., amount to about $100,000. In a word, the State University of Ohio asks the state for the current year for a grant, which together with what it already has would amount to about $500.000. What does it give for the $500,000? It gives excellent instruction unquestionably along certain lines of technical training, but it is also attempting to give instruction in Latin, Greek, Sanscrit, Early Gothic, Indo-Germanic languages. and in fact along all the lines of instruction given in the ordinary college. If this grant were made by the legislature, Cuyahoga county would pay about $3,000 for every student it sends to Columbus. Hamilton county would pay a little more, Lucas county would pay about $1,500, and a number of counties would be assessed for considerable sums of money and not send a single student. On the other hand, Franklin county, with four hundred and three students would pay only a little over $17,000. I cite these statistics simply as an illustration to show what I believe it is possible for the State of Ohio to do in the solution of this question. As I have already said, it can control the public schools, establishing the amount of instruction which they must give. It can establish rules directing under what conditions instruction may be given by the state in public schools preparatory to college. I have already said that I do not believe it can control the instruction which is given in the endowed institutions with which the state is so amply provided, but being so amply provided with instruction along lines of classical training in endowed colleges, the state can, with great advantage to itself give instruction in directions so sadly needed at the present time. The instruction which the state is giving in the development of agriculture is most desirable. Let it increase the quality and scope of the work which it gives in mathematics, electrical, mechanical and civil engineering; let it give higher instruction in the manufacture of pottery, so that we shall be able not only to produce the pottery which we do at the present time, but to produce porcelains which will rival any in the world. We have material and we have gas, so that the advantages which we possess in the manufacture of porcelain and of glass are very great. The state might do a vast amount in other directions.

There is another department in which instruction might be of the greatest value, and that is chemistry. The work which Germany has done in the development of chemistry in the last thirty years is enormous. It has produced for her a colossal revenue. There is no reason why Ohio and other states may not develop the investigation of alciloids, anelines, pigments, perfumes and oils, and undertake research work which will be of incalculable value to the material development of the states. To illustrate what I mean I shall give a concrete example. About twelve years ago Lima oil sold for forty cents a barrel. The Standard Oil Company undertook to refine it, and spent for this purpose about $4,000,000, and when it had spent that sum it had utterly failed to accomplish its purpose. When it failed the price of Lima oil went down to fourteen cents a barrel, and the oil was used only for fuel. An able chemist, whom many of you know, a graduate of Heidelberg University, undertook the investigation of the refining of Lima oil. For less than one-tenth of the sum already spent for the same purpose, which had resulted in failure, he demonstrated to the Standard Oil Company how successfully to refine the oil. The Standard Oil Company had on hand before this time about 15,000,000 barrels of crude Lima oil, which had cost it forty cents per barrel, and the price had gone down to fourteen cents. Before it was known that a process for refining Lima oil had been invented, the Standard Oil Company had bought colossal producing properties upon the basis of fourteen cents a barrel. It sold out in Pennsylvania where crude oil cost $2.40 a barrel, and it was refining Lima oil a year upon the fourteen cent basis before it was known that it was able to do so. This is the reason why the Standard Oil Company is able to pay a dividend of 48 per cent. It is because it has a well educated chemist. If any thoughtful man stops and thinks for a moment what the result to the state has been he must be greatly impressed by it. For the last twelve years the price of Lima oil has varied from fourteen cents to $1.80 a barrel. It sells now at ninety cents a barrel. Its average price during that time has been about one dollar a barrel. Comparing the average price during that period with that obtained before it could be refined, there is a difference of eighty-six cents. The production of Lima oil in the state is about 60,000 barrels per day; in other words, Lima oil produces in the State of Ohio at its present price about $50,000 a day more than it did before it was known that it could be refined. It seems to me that it must be apparent to any man that if a high degree of technical knowledge can produce such colossal results to the state it should be the function of the state to give technical instruction. I might cite other things of equal importance. The same chemist undertook the production of sulphur in the sulphur fields of Louisiana. By the process of forcing into beds of sulphur lying about 600 feet below the surface of the ground, water heated up to about 350° F., he was able to fuse the sulphur and force it to the surface and by this process produce sulphur at $2.80 per ton which is sold at $18.50 a ton. A few years ago the only salt produced in the State of Ohio was that produced down along the Ohio River. It was of low grade and small in quantity. The amount in 1880 was 530,000 barrels. In 1891 this had decreased to 218,000 barrels. The same chemist has invented a process which has made the State of Ohio, incredible as it may seem to you, the second salt producing state in the Union, with an output of 1,600,000 barrels. Salt is now produced with impurities amounting to only one-tenth of one per cent. I firmly believe that the consideration of facts such as these might properly lead the State of Ohio, in the instruction which is subsidized and provided for by the state, practically to solve the question of the relationship of the school, college and university, by regulating the instruction in the common schools, by directing under what conditions instruction preparatory to college work may be given in the public schools and by subsidizing true university education. In addition to this the state should give instruction along technical lines, such as have been indicated. For this no adequate provision now exists, nor is there reasonable hope that the vast expenditure necessary to the highest grade of instruction in technical subjects can be provided in any other way.

To instruction in technical subjects might be added instruction in forestry, in agriculture and in certain of the mechanical arts. It seems to me that the opportunity before this state, before Indiana, and before other states similarly circumstanced with these is unique and most fortunate. I do not believe that the advantage which exists in these states has been by any means realized. It is incomparably beyond those which exist in almost any other state in the Union. Can you imagine that the State of Massachusetts will undertake the establishment of a state university to parallel those branches of instruction which are already so well taught at Harvard, Williams, Amherst, Clark University and the School of Technology of Boston? I do not believe that it would be possible for the state by legislation to secure funds for the purpose. On the other hand, without questioning the greatness of universities such as those of Michigan, Wisconsin and California, we must remember that these universities are in states which are not provided with endowed colleges as are some other states, particularly the State of Ohio. The development of these state institutions is limited by the fact that inasmuch as the state is not provided by private munificence, with thoroughly equipped colleges, giving all the necessary advantages of training along academic and philosophical lines, all this must be provided by the university, and as a result it must give instruction in all languages, both living and dead, and in some that have been for a long time buried. It must give instruction in all the technical lines and in professional lines as well. Here it meets the difficulty of being compelled to provide, for instance in medicine, instruction for students of the old school sometimes called allopathic and also for students of homeopathy. When there is a sufficiently large lobby in the legislature to accomplish it, it is not at all improbable that it will take up various other lines of instruction, such as osteopathy, and no one knows where the thing may terminate. These states must establish schools of dentistry, of law, and it is impossible to say to what degree the division of instruction may not be developed. In states such as Ohio, however, this is unnecessary, but the state may do a thing which is of vastly greater moment. It may establish great laboratories of an efficiency which no ordinary college can possibly provide, and give instruction which is far more advanced than is possible for other states in which all of the instruction along both college and university lines must be provided for. I cannot conceive of any better step for the State of Ohio than to develop higher instruction in the state university, and since the state is not hampered by expenditure incident to many other institutions it will be quite an easy matter to develop here a university which must have recognition not only in this state but in the United States, and we may well say throughout the world. An institution thus developed can command the cordial support of every college in the state, and every citizen would feel in it the greatest pride and would willingly be taxed for its support.

So far as the last proposition before us is concerned, if the division of instruction by the state is desirable and practical, the question arises, Is it legal? As I have already said, this is a part of the question which seems to me more appropriately left to the consideration of my colleague. My own feeling with reference to it is that it is questionable if any action of the sort by the federal government would be possible. I also question if mandatory action by the state directing the course of instruction could constitutionally be brought to bear upon the corporate colleges now existing. It seems to me, however, that the State of Ohio may, as I have indicated, do a vast amount toward the development of successful instruction and make the state as great in its intellectual as it has come to be in its political and commercial development.

What is true of this state is equally true of other states similarly situated. As it seems to me, institutions of instruction, whether they are supported by the state or by private munificence, whether they are for primary or advanced instruction, have but one reason for existence, and that is, that they employ the student's time to the best possible advantage. At the present time in the total absence of any correlation in the teaching of our various schools, much valuable time is lost and much instruction is but inadequately given. I thoroughly believe that the time has arrived when the State of Ohio, and others similarly circumstanced, may secure the ends so much to be desired, viz., that all teaching which is done shall be done well; that it shall meet certain established standards to obtain recognition by the state, and that instruction shall be provided in technical lines upon a plane higher than that which exists anywhere else in the world. If the state cannot legally determine the standing of all its schools, both public and private, it can regulate the standard of instruction in its common and high schools, and it can support a school of technical instruction upon so high a plane as to command the enthusiastic support of every citizen and every college of the state.

PROFESSOR DENNEY, of Ohio State University, commenting on Professor Allen's paper, said that the statistics quoted were misleading and inaccurate so far as they referred to Ohio State University. A large number of students charged to Franklin county really belonged to other counties, some being members of families who had but recently come to Columbus in order to educate their children, others having enrolled themselves as Franklin county students in order to secure voting privileges. A fairer numerical test of the usefulness of a university would be afforded by asking, not "Where do the students come from?" but "Where are the graduates and ex-students now located and what service are they rendering to the state?" Cleveland might not send very many students to the state university at present, but Cleveland had many graduates and ex-students of the university in its citizenship who were filling important places as engineers, teachers, editors, and professional men. The geographical origin of the students should never determine whether or not a state university should be supported.

The opposition to the Ohio State University was centered against the college of arts, philosophy and science, not against the colleges of engineering and agriculture. He desired to call attention to the fact that the additional money now being asked for by the Ohio State University was for engineering buildings. Yet the appropriation was being opposed by those who said they wanted a great engineering college at the university. As dean of the college of arts, he would like to know how a great college of engineering could be carried on without professors of modern languages, and how the university could continue to receive the federal appropriation unless it continued to teach history, economics, and the English language, as commanded in the second Morrill bill. The Massachusetts Institute of Technology had found that it must provide general courses, such as are offered in any college of liberal arts, in order to meet the proper demands upon a great engineering school.

Before the college of arts, philosophy and science was abolished for "paralleling and paralyzing" the work of other Ohio colleges, he would like to know how a great graduate school at the university such as was advocated by the other Ohio colleges could be maintained without retaining a good share of the advanced undergraduate work now offered in the college of arts. To abolish a college of liberal arts as the first step towards establishing a great graduate school seemed to him to be illogical. Clark University and Johns Hopkins, which had started without undergraduate departments, had been compelled to institute them afterwards in the interest of sound graduate work.

In his opinion the colleges of Ohio should keep before them the fact that a very small percentage of young people of college age were in college. The effort should therefore be not to curtail the usefulness of any existing institution, state or private; each institution should do the work that it could do best; there was work enough for all. Each institution should be allowed to develop along natural lines according to the demands of its constituency; and it followed that if students were permitted to go where they desired, the institutions that did the best work need have no fears. As for the Ohio State University what it asked of the friends of education in Ohio was, most especially, to let it alone a few years. In his opinion the natural course of events would soon solve many of the problems that had been raised by Professor Allen.

The discussion was continued by Dean E. H. Hopkins of Western Reserve University, who considered the question with special reference to the high school.

In the absence of Professor Stagg the following paper was read by Professor J. V. Denney:

THE USES OF FOOTBALL.

BY PROFESSOR A. A. STAGG, OF THE UNIVERSITY OF
CHICAGO.

American football may very properly be called the greatest of all athletic games. It comprises more science and art and more physical, mental and moral qualities than any other sport. It is one of the most exacting games physically, and yet one of the most healthful. By its very vigor it sets up a bar to the feeble and sickly engaging in it. It is a game for healthy, robust youth—fit to be played only during the bracing weather of the autumn season.

Under no circumstances should it be engaged in seriously without suitable preliminary preparation physically for it. Played by boys and young men after such preparation it yields marvelous returns physically, mentally and morally.

I need not speak of the physical returns other than to say that young men build up large, strong and elastic frames and muscle faster through playing football than from any of the other sports.

As to the mental development I may say it is a game of wits—and wits every second of play. There is no time during the play when a player's mind is not at work. Calm and clear thinking must tell him the signal, must indicate the point of attack, must interpret his part in it in general, and his judgment, strategy and tactics in particular. The changes are kaleidoscopic in frequency and variety, and call for instantaneous perception, judgment and action. Quick decision and adjustment follow in close and frequent sequence.

Football also trains players to lose self-consciousness; to be calm under excitement and yet constantly on the alert; to develop concentration and yet to be resourceful.

But if football is a game of wits it is also a game of character. The grandest traits of human character are obedience to duty and loyalty to a principle, a fellow-being, an organization, an institution, a country. Without these every state would be a state of anarchy, every home the nest bed of anarchy, every man an anarchist. Better than any book of moral science or code of ethics football develops this grand moral sense. Obedience to daily practice, obedience to coaching, obedience to training rules, to discipline, to self-denial, to frequent physical discomfort in correcting faults of play or in learning new methods of attack and defense, obedience to the various responsibilities of team work, obedience to the sense of duty to the team, to the institution for which it stands —these and all these with unvarying monotony are ever present in playing the game.

Football develops the ability to feel and to bear responsibility. Individual responsibility is the keynote of the play, team play the harmony. Every man must be in line and act on time. Eleven men must be in every play. Each has his special function. He can not, he must not, he will not, shirk it. He is a link in the chain, a cog in the wheel—aye! he is much more, he is a thinking link, an adjustable cog, with great possibilities for tremendous individual initiative.

Boys learn to know this relationship and to feel this responsibility and to bear it. They can not comprehend the game ever so slightly without having it impressed upon them. Every kick-off, every line-up, every scrimmage, every signal, every play constantly and persistently deepens this impression.

It is said that "atmosphere, not dogma, educates." Surely then the never-ceasing sense of responsibility and duty which surrounds the football player can not fail to quicken and to deepen his moral senses.

While football lays emphasis on team play it is to a

peculiar degree a game of individuals, and for the development of individuals. At every scrimmage the rush line feels this, at every charge and defence the backs are aware of it. It is the old battle—man against man, and every player soon learns that he is up against it, as it were. Every man will fight when he gets into a corner, and in a football game he gets there pretty often. Then again the game demands of every player that he do certain particular things at certain particular times. He must do them oftentimes entirely himself. Certain features of the play are entirely his. Duty, responsibility, everything urge him on. He does them. Again and again he does them, and like the baby learning to walk, each step which he takes gives him strength and confidence in himself. Self-reliance gained even in playing football opens up avenues of endeavor which are unending in their possibilities.

Still further, I believe there is more moral fibre built upon the atheletic field than in any of the other affairs which take a boy's attention. Let me give you a concrete illustration: A boy takes part in a football game for the first time. He is quick-tempered. In the midst of a scrimmage perhaps he is jostled by some one, and his attention is quickly turned from the play in hand, which had been all absorbing, and he immediately seeks retaliation on the one who has given him the bump. This happens again and again, and as often does his temper get the better of him. But after a while, he notices that each time he gives way in temper and turns his attention to retaliating, he gives his opponents so much greater chance to carry out their purposes, and finally he learns to grit his teeth and stand it, because he sees that it pays to keep his attention centered on the play in hand. The boy has learned an invaluable lesson for life, namely, that one cannot afford to lose control of himself, because it interferes with the attainment of the desired end; ultimately, because it is strong to be master of himself.

But then there is another side of self-control which must not be overlooked, and that is the self-control which comes from training in contests. It is most beneficent in its results. It is right in line also with the teaching and practice of the old church fathers. The object is not to make the body so healthy and pure and strong that it may be a fit temple for the indwelling of the Holy Spirit, but no priest or church father could have prescribed a course of dieting and regularity of living which could do more for the body than the courses of training which the young men undergo in athletic teams. And the result is surprising in its helpfulness to purity and healthfulness of living, and in the power of self-control which the young men gain And after all, the power most needed in a young man's life is self-control, or the ability to keep the body in balance—to be its master while it works for his highest and best interests.

Can any one place a value on the power of such training and exercise on a young man's life? It is inestimable. Only those who have passed through a period of such training can form any idea of its helpfulness. and even they do not know its full influence on their lives. The baser thoughts have little to do with a brain washed with such rich, pure blood. The passions have little sway over a man with that fineness of physical feeling, with those steady nerves, and with that spontaneity and wholesomeness of life.

It is not too much to say that the training that is undergone in football has saved hundreds of young men unto purity and right living, and it has given to a vast number such a physical foundation that it has been possible for them to double and even treble the productiveness of their lives.

The training of the will power which a young man gets on the athletic field is of no small value in this fight. The daily practice of the will which is brought about in

football, where a youth puts forth his utmost efforts to
win, to overcome the points of difficulty which are constantly presented in the contests, to vanquish an opponent,
to crush down the give-up spirit, which frequently arises
when things are going against him or when he becomes
physically tired or fain would stop,—all these efforts train
a youth in the powerful use of his will—even to that extent that he will never give up, for he has trained himself
to conquer all things.

Again, football trains boys to be generous-minded
and unselfish. The whole discipline of the game, while it
cultivates individuality, tends to destroy selfishness. This
is notably true of college football, where the man who does
not subordinate his individual interests for the success of
the college or for the good of the team is cast aside and re-
placed by another. College sentiment, not to mention that
of the team, the captain and the coach, all unite in making
the life of a selfish athlete miserable. The college athlete
who will not deny himself certain luxuries of palate,
and all stimulants and narcotics, will not take on regular habits of eating and sleeping, giving up the delights
of special dinners and spreads and entertainments beyond
hours, and then report for practice regularly and under
direction; who will not utterly forget his own personal interests in the play in hand; that there is a grandstand full
of people watching him; that he has any friends or rela-
tives in the crowd who would be glad to have him with
them during the intervals of play; who will not take des-
perate chances with a disregard of a hard fall and subsequent pain—the college athlete, I say, who will not do all
this and do it willingly and with zest, is usually not wanted
on the best college teams. All this is expected of athletes
and is usually gladly given. In fact, the principle of unselfishness in regard to one's own desires and interests
when college honor and the team would be affected thereby, is one of the most powerful and beautiful expressions

of loyalty to be seen in modern life. Largely on this account, I venture to say, rests the public interest in college sport, because it is at once the highest and best type of amateurism and the essence of loyalty and unselfishness.

I believe in playing football because it develops healthy and manly men—men who will not be afraid of the rough and tumble of life; men of courage, of strength, of self-reliance, of determination and perseverance; men of high moral sense of duty; men of the do-or-die and never-give-up qualities; men who can bear and forbear; who possess the self-control gained in many a scrimmage; who know how to take defeat and accept victory; men who see quickly and as quickly act; who are accustomed to handle emergencies; men of steady nerves, susceptible of the greatest response to the command of the will.

Football trains the individual to see opportunities and to seize them; to take in the existing circumstances and to judge accordingly; to perceive quickly and to interpret rightly; to be strategic and to outwit strategy; to obey authority and to be the leader; to subordinate individual interests for the team's sake, while at the same time it employs the individual to the fullest degree.

THE USE AND ABUSE OF INTERSCHOLASTIC ATHLETICS.

BY PRINCIPAL J. E. ARMSTRONG, OF ENGLEWOOD HIGH SCHOOL, CHICAGO.

I am not an athlete nor do I lay any claim to past athletic honors except that when a boy I could outrun my companions. This ability has served a useful purpose ever since, for, as the old proverb has it, "He who fights and runs away, may live to fight another day." Some of my worthy coadjutors may not so easily escape the wrath of our common foe, for lack of this useful accomplishment.

I have the courage, however, and the war instinct sufficiently developed in me to stand my ground and defend
our position until our opponents surrender or succeed in
spiking our guns.

My interest in athletics is chiefly from a psychological
view point, since I believe that the instincts of young people demand the stimuli which athletic sports offer, and
that to deprive youth of these health-giving stimuli leaves
them dwarfed in manly characteristics and lacking in
some of the fiber that goes to make up a man in the best
sense of the word. I am fully aware of the fact that we
have many specimens of the noblest types of manhood
who have never played a game of football or tennis, but
to say this is simply to repeat the protest against college
education by self-educated men. We are living in a new
age; conditions of life are very different from what they
were when the majority of us were schoolboys. Our life
in crowded cities makes it more necessary than ever to
look carefully after the playtime of our young people or
we shall have a race dwarfed in intellect, weak in will
power, and lacking in manly courage.

Some twenty years ago, when I first began my work
as a teacher in a city high school, it seemed to me something was decidedly lacking in the life of the average boy
and girl of high school age. There were no organized
sports, except possibly baseball. Marbles and tops had
been outgrown. To smoke cigarettes or play pranks on
teachers or younger pupils seemed to be the chief amusement. An occasional fist fight or wild outbreak of rebel-
lion served as the safety valve for pent-up animal spirits.
About ten years ago, our high schools in Chicago became
interested in football, through the example of our neigh-
boring colleges and universities. It was like a burning
match applied to tinder. The schools went wild over it.
The pupils of many of our schools became interested as a
mob in the affairs of their own team. There immediately

sprang up a spirit of loyalty to school and a well defined belligerent attitude toward all rival schools. The girls shared in these feelings quite as much as the boys. This athletic spirit wellnigh overshadowed every other interest. Teachers and parents were at once divided among themselves as to what should be done. Many teachers strenuously advocated suppressing the whole thing. Some said, "If this goes on we shall have to give up Latin. Our pupils have more interest in athletics than they have in the Classics. Let us destroy this heresy." Other teachers went into the field, joined in the spirit and found thereby fresh interest in Cæsar's wars. There was less tendency to mischievous pranks, teasing and bullying than ever before. Schools that countenanced or encouraged athletics found an easy road to the pupils' hearts if not to their intellects.

Many parents appealed to the schools to suppress those brutal games, admitting their inability to prevent their *one* boy from participating, vainly hoping the schools could and would extend their control over the after-school playtime, miles away from the school grounds. Then came the press, feeling after public sentiment: now condemning the schools for encouraging games that disturb the public quiet with shouts of enthusiasm or deafening blasts of horns, and now condemning the schools for trying to interfere with the liberty of pupils after school hours. Even school boards and legislatures have thought to place a ban on some of the more vigorous games by prohibition; but the games go on just the same.

Choosing and getting a wife is not all moonshine nor sunshine, nor does it always prove to be without danger or difficulty. Many suffer defeat or forfeit their lives for their foolish ambition. Yet mankind in general and man in particular is not disheartened at this. It only makes the prize the more to be desired. The schools that saw in the intensity of athletic interest a mysterious power,

8

and an easy road to youthful co-operation, have persevered in their efforts to eliminate the evils and preserve the good. The first attempts at faculty control were met with open hostility. Pupils felt that this was their own affair, and that as athletic sports were conducted after school hours the faculty should have nothing to say about their control. Even some parents and the press took this ground with them; but the difficulties and abuses grew and multiplied. Money was required to provide suits, balls and coaches, and the faculty must be appealed to for funds. Semi-professional athletes or "ringers" entered the "other fellow's" school, and some one in authority was needed to show the injustice of this. Of course no school complained of its own bad practice. Athletic leagues made regulations for correcting abuses. but found great difficulty in enforcing them. A protest was usually made against each winning team, and, naturally, all the defeated teams would vote against the team that had in turn defeated each of them; so, many times, victory was voted out of existence by the power of the ballot.

In the next stage of the game, the intensity of the struggle for athletic honors knew no bounds. Young men of athletic ability enrolled in the schools, played football, won the applause of the assembled multitudes, failed in all their studies and left school at the end of the football season covered with glory. When the emergency arose, as it frequently did, a "ringer" was taken in under an assumed name, and while he did not go home with glory to his real name, he frequently went with more spending money in his pocket.

Some schools saw early the necessity of making a scholarship rule, but this worked great hardship, since many of the opposing teams were under no such rules. Three of the Chicago high schools whose teams were most prominent in athletics were called together by the writer, and, after a general plan was formed, representatives of the other high schools of Chicago and Cook county were invited, and an athletic league was formed which superseded the former pupil organization. Rules were adopted governing the eligibility of players and providing for a faculty board of control who should hear and decide all protests. Since that time improvements have been made in the management of all athletic sports so that few abuses remain. Supt. Cooley deserves great credit for adding the final touch of authority needed to bring about the desired condition of perfect faculty control. I do not mean by this that there are no difficulties to overcome. That "eternal vigilance is the price of liberty" is as true here as elsewhere. I do believe, however, that school athletics have now passed from the experimental stage to a settled condition of control, thoughtful supervision and healthy development, and while some are still hoping that public sentiment will rise up and with one mighty stroke of legislative enactment make football as safe as marbles and bathing, as devoid of risk as a sponge bath, others will go on as they have in the past, utilizing the mighty force of instinctive love of play to lead young people to make the most of themselves during the years of preparation for the mighty conflict of life.

Away back in the mist-shrouded ages of prehistoric human existence, man disputed with the hyena and the cave bear for supremacy; later on, and, alas, too near to the present, he has disputed with his fellow man for the same. War has occupied so large a share of the interests of the race that history consists chiefly of battles, victories and defeats. No one who has made a study of heredity will deny that those occupations that have chiefly concerned a race of animals cannot help but impress the progeny with strong instinctive tendencies. Is it strange, then, that our children naturally resist authority, become wayward and contrary, rebel against control, quarrel, or fight? These are the traits of character that led our

Anglo-Saxon forefathers to become the liberty-loving, independent men they were, and we honor them for it. Are we surprised that the ten-year-old boy goes wild over the stories of war and carnage, or marches all day long with a wooden gun and a tin bayonet, and with a feather in his cap? Who does not recall with a thrill of pleasure even now the lines:

> "Oh! were you ne'er a school boy,
> And did you never train,
> And feel that swelling of the heart
> You ne'er can feel again?
>
> Didst never meet far down the street,
> With plume and banner gay,
> When the kettle for the kettle-drum
> Bade you march, march away?"

It is our Roman inheritance that makes us like organization and submission to a leader. This is the time for lessons in saluting "old glory," for loud booming firecrackers and other such forms of patriotism. Deprive the boy of these stimuli and you will scarcely, if at all, awaken the same degree of enthusiastic devotion to the old flag. About the same time in the boy's life he becomes a tease. He tortures his pet animals or his smaller playmates. This occupation becomes fascinating because it makes him seem stronger than those who wince under his treatment. Later on the boy becomes an Indian fighter or a pirate. He breaks windows, smashes fences or pulls up shrubbery or paints things red. It gives him a feeling of power to see things crumble or vanish. But this power to destroy is only the complement of the power to create. Give him the power to create some of the vagaries of fancy, show him his limitations from the lack of skill, show him what skill guided by intelligence can do and he becomes a devotee to the arts and crafts. Manual training is the demand of this instinct.

Then there follow the instincts of the age of Chivalry,

when man was "The Lover, sighing like furnace, with a woful ballad, made to his mistress' eyebrow." No more uncombed hair or untidy clothes. He now seeks to please those he formerly sought to annoy. A new fire burns within and love is life. His war instinct assumes a new form. He is desirous of the trophies of war. He would adorn his fair lady with medals and badges won in contest. He desires to become a leader, and would like to organize the scattered and wasted forces. He is even willing to become a part of a greater whole or a cog in the wheel in order to accomplish greater results. This is the age for football and other team games. This is the time to teach submission to law, concentration, devotion to leadership, self-restraint and self-denial.

Social games of all kinds recognize the war instinct. Karl Groos traces the fighting play from its most cruel manifestation to its culmination in tragedy. Colin Scott says, "In some tribes a man dare not marry, and indeed no woman would have him, until he has slain a certain number of foes." Groos says, "It is not the cruelty of destructiveness but the feeling of power in combat that is most prominent in tragedy."

Life is indeed a warfare from that of the brute to the highest intellectual and spiritual being. Can there be anything more pitiable than the young man who has been so tied to his mother's apron that he cannot look the world in the face for fear his feelings will be hurt?—one who dares not mingle with men and women because he is too sensitive to ridicule? He needs the jibes and taunts and tricks of full-blooded, vigorous boys to thicken his mental skin and arouse in him some of the instinct of war before he will become of service to society or humanity. Compare this pitiable creature with the young man trained in play warfare, alert, keen, resourceful, accustomed to give and take the sally of wit.—which is but the warfare of words,—courageous and withal manly.

Have we not too long made a mistake in allowing these instincts to develop without recognizing their purpose? Spaulding points out the fact that the instincts of the chick, when allowed to react to proper stimuli, establish habits that persist throughout life to protect the life of the individual. On the other hand, when the proper stimulus is withheld, the instinct soon fades and the resultant habit is lost forever. If we could but utilize these mighty forces in training youth, we might establish habits that would be of infinite value to the race. We may so starve the instinct for war that our young men will despise the struggle for advancement, or for victory of any kind, and become the lifeless, ambitionless, idle beings we call tramps, loafers or drones.

You may ask if football is to cure all this. No, that would be an extravagant claim. I firmly believe, however, that football furnishes the strongest stimulus and offers the best training to the war instinct; that many other athletic games stand nearly as high in furnishing this stimulus; that instead of opposing these sports we should rather assist the boys in eliminating the evils or abuses. We should teach them that in this warfare their antagonists are not their enemies; that it would be better to be defeated than win by unfair means; and above all they must be just and manly at all times. In order to bring this about the faculty of the schools should unite to make proper conditions: to make rules uniform; to make proper boards of appeal; to provide police protection against the hoodlum element that frequent all games where skill or chance may offer an opportunity to indulge a depraved phase of the war instinct; to procure proper officials and see that all necessary machinery is provided to remove temptations and prevent unfair tactics.

Many of the states now have state athletic associations conducted by the faculties of the schools. There are many schools throughout these states, however, that would rather leave these matters to chance than recognize the games as a part of the education of youth. They escape some annoyance but neglect a great opportunity to shape the lives of the pupils entrusted to their care. Not until we recognize the power of the war instinct in preparing young people for life's battles shall we rise to the fullest possibilities in training future men and women. War plays must ever be the means of awakening dormant powers, and the schools and colleges should see that the instincts of youth are utilized in their fullest preparation for life's more serious warfare.

What I would plead for, then, is not that athletics should be treated as a necessary evil, and certainly not that they should be suppressed as being opposed to education, but that schools should recognize that contests of all kinds, and especially physical contests, are the manifestations of the war instinct of the race; that the war instinct is useful in establishing the spirit of contest, struggle with opposing circumstances, the desire to overcome obstacles; and that it leads to the principle of organization and concentration of social forces. I would plead for more careful supervision on the part of the faculties of the schools, just recognition of the interests of youth, and a high standard of manly conduct. And while the victory may seem to be the goal in plain sight or the championship banner, the real victory will be a victory over self, the goal of full preparation for life's contests and the pennant of justice, liberality and noble manhood.

On motion of Principal Harris it was voted that a committee* consisting of three representatives from the

---

*The following persons were appointed to serve as members of this committee: Principal E. L. Harris, of the Central High School, Cleveland; Principal J. E. Armstrong, of Englewood High School, Chicago; Principal C. G. Ballou of the Toledo High School; Professor A. A. Stagg of the University of Chicago; Professor J. V. Denney of Ohio State University; and Professor C. S. Slichter, of the University of Wisconsin.

colleges and three from the high schools, be raised to take into consideration questions relating to both interscholastic and intercollegiate contests, and to formulate a uniform set of rules to regulate such contests.

The report of the auditing committee was then presented as follows, and, upon motion, was adopted:

Your auditing committee beg leave to report that they have examined the accounts of the treasurer for the year 1901–1902, and find them correctly cast, with adequate vouchers for all expenditures.

F. L. BLISS,
C. E. ST. JOHN.

The committee on the time and place of the next meeting then reported as follows:

Your committee recommend that the Association meet in 1903 in Chicago, at about one year from this time, the exact date of the meeting being left to the Executive Committee.

JOSEPH SWAIN,
E. W. COY,
J. H. MACCRACKEN,

The report was adopted.

The committee appointed to nominate officers for the ensuing year, reported as follows:

The Committee on Nominations beg leave to submit the following list of officers of the Association for the ensuing year:

FOR PRESIDENT:

Director Geo. N. Carman,
    Lewis Institute, Chicago.

FOR VICE PRESIDENTS:

OHIO—

President Chas. F. Thwing,
    Western Reserve University, Cleveland.
Principal E. W. Coy,
    Hughes High School, Cincinnati.

MICHIGAN—

Professor F. W. Kelsey,
University of Michigan, Ann Arbor.
Principal F. L. Bliss,
The University School, Detroit.

INDIANA—

President Joseph Swain,
Indiana University, Bloomington.
Superintendent Edward Ayres,
Lafayette.

ILLINOIS—

President W. R. Harper,
University of Chicago.
Dr. A. F. Nightingale,
Chicago.

WISCONSIN—

Professor E. A. Birge,
University of Wisconsin, Madison.
A. W. Tressler,
Inspector of High Schools, Madison.

MINNESOTA—

Professor W. N. West,
University of Minnesota, Minneapolis.
President F. A. Weld,
Normal School, Moorhead.

OWA—

President William F. King,
Cornell College, Mt. Vernon.
President H. H. Seerley,
State Normal School, Cedar Falls.

MISSOURI—

Professor M. S. Snow,
Washington University, St. Louis.
Principal W. J. S. Bryan,
High School, St. Louis.

NEBRASKA—

President E. B. Andrews,
University of Nebraska, Lincoln.
Principal H. J. Davenport,
High School, Lincoln.

KANSAS—

Professor F. H. Snow,
University of Kansas, Lawrence.
Superintendent W. A. Davidson,
Topeka.

COLORADO—
> President James H. Baker,
>> University of Colorado, Boulder.
> Principal Wm. H. Smiley,
>> High School No. 1, Denver.

FOR SECRETARY—
> Professor F. N. Scott,
>> University of Michigan, Ann Arbor.

FOR TREASURER—
> Principal J. E. Armstrong,
>> Englewood High School, Chicago.

FOR MEMBERS OF EXECUTIVE COMMITTEE, in addition to th
President, Secretary, and Treasurer, *ex officio*:

Professor C. A. Waldo, Purdue University, Lafayette, Indiana.
Principal E. L. Harris, Central High School, Cleveland.
President J. R. Kirk, State Normal School, Kirksville, Missouri.
President G. E. McLean, University of Iowa, Iowa City.

Signed by the Committee $\begin{cases} \text{A. S. DRAPER,} \\ \text{S. O. HARTWELL,} \\ \text{T. H. JOHNSTON.} \end{cases}$

The report was adopted.

The following resolution was adopted by unanimous vote
of the Association.

Resolved, That the members of this Association extend
their hearty thanks to President Thwing, Superintenden
Jones, Principal Harris and their efficient body of assistants
who have so cordially received and entertained the North
Central Association of Colleges and Secondary Schools at this
seventh annual meeting in Cleveland, and who have so mate
rially and vitally contributed to the success of the meeting.

We also desire to express our appreciation of the kindnes
of the Chamber of Commerce and the officers of Beckwith
Church in granting the use of their respective buildings for the
meetings of the Association.

The following persons and institutions were, upon recom
mendation by the executive committee, admitted to member
ship in the Association:

Institutional members: University School, Cleveland,

Ohio (Principal George D. Pettee); East High School, Cleveland, Ohio (Principal B. U. Rannells); South High School, Cleveland, Ohio (Principal G. A. Ruetenik); Lincoln High School, Cleveland, Ohio (Principal J. W. McLane); High School, Chillicothe, Ohio (Principal Ralph R. Upton); East High School, Columbus, Ohio (Principal F. B. Pearson); Park College, Parkville, Missouri (President Lowell M. McAfee).

Individual members: Professor T. F. Moran, Purdue University, Lafayette, Indiana; Professor Charles S. Howe, Case School of Applied Science, Cleveland, Ohio; Professor U. S. Grant, Northwestern University, Evanston, Illinois.

The Association then adjourned.

At the close of the meeting the members of the Association through the courtesy of President Thwing, took luncheon at Guilford House, College for Women, Western Reserve University.

LIST OF MEMBERS, 1902 AND 1903.

Institutions.

(c. m. means charter member.)

OHIO.

Ohio State University, c. m., Columbus, President W. O. Thompson.
Western Reserve University, c. m., Cleveland, President Chas F. Thwing.
Oberlin College, c. m., Oberlin, President H. C. King.
Ohio Wesleyan University, c. m., Delaware, President Jas. W. Bashford.
Denison University, '99, Granville, President D. B. Purinton.
University of Cincinnati, '99, Cincinnati, President H. Ayers.
Central High School, c. m., Cleveland, Principal Edward L. Harris.
Hughes High School, '96, Cincinnati, Principal E. W. Coy.
Steele High School, '96, Dayton, Principal Malcolm Booth.
High School, '96, Toledo, Principal C. G. Ballou.
Walnut Hills High School, '99, Cincinnati, Principal J. Remsen Bishop.
Woodward High School, '99, Cincinnati, Principal Geo. W. Harper.
West High School, '00, Cleveland, Principal Theo. H. Johnston.
East High School, '02, Columbus, Principal F. B. Pearson.
University School, '02, Cleveland, Principal George D. Pettee.
South High School, '02, Cleveland, Principal G. A. Ruetenik.
Lincoln High School, '02, Cleveland, Principal J. W. McLane.
High School, '02, Chillicothe, Principal Ralph R. Upton.
East High School, Cleveland, Principal B. U. Rannels.

MICHIGAN.

University of Michigan, c. m., Ann Arbor, President Jas. B. Angell.
Albion College, c. m., Albion, President Samuel Dickie.
Central High School, c. m., Grand Rapids, Principal A. J. Volland.
Michigan Military Academy, c. m., Orchard Lake.
High School, '95, Kalamazoo, Superintendent S. O. Hartwell.
East Side High School, '95, Saginaw, Superintendent E. C. Warriner.
University School, '00, Detroit, Principal Frederick L. Bliss.

INDIANA.

Indiana University, c. m., Bloomington, President Joseph Swain.
Wabash College, c. m., Crawfordsville, President W. P. Kane.
High School, c. m., LaPorte, Superintendent J. W. Knight.
High School, '96, Fort Wayne, Principal C. F. Lane.
Girls' Classical School, '00, Indianapolis, Principal May W. Sewall.
High School, '01, Lafayette.

ILLINOIS.

University of Illinois, c. m., Champaign, President Andrew S. Draper.

University of Chicago, c. m., Chicago, President Wm. R. Harper.

Northwestern University, c. m., Evanston, President E. J. James.

Lake Forest University, c. m., Lake Forest, President R. D. Harlan.

Knox College, '96, Galesburg, Professor H. E. Griffith.

High School, c. m., Evanston, Principal Henry L. Boltwood.

Northwestern Academy, c. m., Evanston, Principal H. F. Fisk.

Morgan Park Academy, c. m., Morgan Park, Dean W. J. Chase.

Manual Training School, c. m., Chicago, Director H. H. Belfield.

Harvard School, c. m., Chicago, Principal John J. Schobinger.

High School, c. m., Peoria, Superintendent Newton C. Dougherty.

Lake Forest Academy, c. m., Lake Forest, Principal Conrad Hibbeler.

North Division High School, '96, Chicago, Principal O. S. Westcott.

West Division High School, '96, Chicago, Principal C. M. Clayberg.

Hyde Park High School, '95, Chicago, Principal C. W. French.

Lake View High School, '96, Chicago, Principal B. F. Buck.

Englewood High School, '96, Chicago, Principal J. E. Armstrong.

Ottawa Tp. High School, '96, Ottawa, Principal J. O. Leslie.

Lyons Tp. High School, '96, La Grange, Principal Cole.

Lewis Institute, '95, Chicago, Director G. N. Carman.

Streator Tp. High School, '97, Streator, Principal Alfred Bayliss.

Bradley Polytechnic Institute, '97, Peoria, Director E. O. Sisson.

High School, '98, Elgin, Principal Eugene C. Pierce.

Lake High School, '99, Chicago, Principal Edward F. Stearns.

Marshall High School, '99, Chicago, Principal Louis J. Block.

Ferry Hall Seminary, '00, Lake Forest, Principal Sabra L. Sargent.

WISCONSIN.

University of Wisconsin, c. m., Madison, President Chas. K. Adams.[1]

Beloit College, c. m., Beloit, President Edward D. Eaton.

Milwaukee-Downer College, '97, Milwaukee, President Ellen C. Sabin.

Milwaukee Academy, '97, Milwaukee, Principal J. H. Pratt.

MINNESOTA.

University of Minnesota, '96, Minneapolis, President Cyrus Northrup.

IOWA.

State University of Iowa, c. m., Iowa City, President Geo. E. MacLean.

Cornell College, c. m., Mt. Vernon, President Wm. F. King.

State Normal School, c. m., Cedar Falls, President Homer H. Seerley.

Iowa College, '95, Grinnell, President J. H. P. Main.

High School, '01, Muscatine.

---

1 Deceased.

MISSOURI.

University of Missouri, c. m., Columbia, President Richard H. Jesse.

Washington University, c. m., St. Louis, Chancellor Winfield S. Chaplin.

Drury College, '98, Springfield, President Homer T. Fuller.

Missouri Valley College, '98, Marshall, President Wm. H. Black.

High School, '96, St. Louis, Principal Wm. J. S. Bryan.

Westminster College, '00, Fulton, President John H. MacCracken.

Mexico High School, '00, Mexico, Superintendent D. A. McMillan.

Manual Training High School, '00, Kansas City, Principal G. B. Morrison.

Mary Institute, '00, St. Louis, Principal E. H. Sears.

Kirkwood High School, '00, Kirkwood, Superintendent R. G. Kinkead.

Park College, '02, Parkville, President Lowell M. McAfee.

NEBRASKA.

University of Nebraska, '96, Lincoln, President E. Benj. Andrews.

KANSAS.

University of Kansas, '96, Lawrence, Chancellor Frank Strong.

COLORADO.

University of Colorado, '96, Boulder, President Jas. H. Baker.

Colorado College, '96, Colorado Springs, President W. F. Slocum.

High School No. 1, '96, Denver, Principal Wm. H. Smiley.

OKLAHOMA.

University of Oklahoma, '01, Norman, President David R. Boyd.

Individual Members.

OHIO.

Cady Staley, '95, President Case School, Cleveland.

Henry C. King, '96, Professor in Oberlin College, Oberlin.

Charles S. Howe, '02, Professor in Case School of Applied Science. Cleveland.

MICHIGAN.

W. W. Beman, '95, Professor in the University of Michigan, Ann Arbor.

Francis W. Kelsey, '95, Professor in the University of Michigan, Ann Arbor.

Fred N. Scott, '98, Professor in the University of Michigan, Ann Arbor.

L. H. Jones, '95, President of State Normal, Ypsilanti.

INDIANA.

Clarence A. Waldo, '95, Professor in Purdue University, Lafayette.

Carl Leo Mees, '96, President of Rose Polytechnic, Terre Haute.

J. J. Mills, '99, President of Earlham College, Richmond.
Robert J. Aley, '99, Professor in Indiana University, Bloomington.
Edward Ayers, '99, Superintendent of Schools, Lafayette.
W. W. Parsons, '99, President of the State Normal School, Terre Haute.
Stanley Coulter, '01, Professor in Purdue University, Lafayette.
C. N. Kendall, '01, Superintendent of Schools, Indianapolis.
T. F. Moran, '02, Professor in Purdue University, Lafayette.

ILLINOIS.

S. A. Forbes, Dean, University of Illinois, Champaign.
A. V. E. Young, '95, Professor in Northwestern University, Evanston.
Thomas C. Chamberlin, '95, Professor in the University of Chicago, Chicago.
Harry P. Judson, '95, Professor in the University of Chicago, Chicago.
Marion Talbot, '97, Dean of Women, University of Chicago, Chicago.
Wm. A. Greeson, '97, Dean of Lewis Institute, Chicago.
F. W. Gunsaulus, '96, President of Armour Institute, Chicago.
U. S. Grant, '02, Professor in Northwestern University, Evanston.
Thomas F. Holgate, '99, Professor in Northwestern University, Evanston.
J. A. James, Professor in Northwestern University, Evanston.
A. F. Nightingale, c. m., Chicago.

WISCONSIN.

Edward A. Birge, '96, Professor in the University of Wisconsin, Madison.
M. V. O'Shea, '98, Professor in the University of Wisconsin, Madison.
John B. Johnson, '99, Professor in the University of Wisconsin, Madison.[1]

MINNESOTA.

George B. Aiton, '97, State Inspector of High Schools, Minneapolis.

MISSOURI.

F. Louis Soldan, '00, Superintendent of Schools, St. Louis.
John R. Kirk, '98, President of the State Normal School, Kirksville.
C. M. Woodward, '99, Professor in Washington University, St. Louis.

KANSAS.

W. A. Davidson, '99, Superintendent of Schools, Topeka.

CONSTITUTION OF THE NORTH CENTRAL ASSOCIATION OF COLLEGES AND SECONDARY SCHOOLS.

AS AMENDED AT THE THIRD ANNUAL MEETING, APRIL 1, 1898.

ARTICLE I.

NAME.

The name of this Association shall be the North Central Association of Colleges and Secondary Schools.

ARTICLE II.

OBJECT.

The object of the Association shall be to establish closer relations between the colleges and secondary schools of the North Central States.

ARTICLE III.

MEMBERSHIP.

Section 1.—The members of the Association shall consist of the following two classes: First, colleges and universities, and secondary schools. Secondly, individuals identified with educational work within the limits of the Association.

Sec. 2.—Election to membership shall require a two-thirds vote of the members present at any meeting, and shall be made only upon the nomination of the Executive Committee.

Sec. 3.—In the membership of the Association, the representation of higher and of secondary education shall be as nearly equal as possible.

Sec. 4.—An institutional member shall be represented at the meeting of the Association by its executive head, or by some one designated by him in credentials addressed to the Secretary.

Sec. 5.—No college or university shall be eligible to membership whose requirements for admission represent less than four years of secondary work.

Sec. 6.—No college or university shall be eligible to membership which confers the degree of Doctor of Philosophy or Doctor of Science except after a period of three years of graduate study, not less than two of which shall be years of resident study, one of which shall be at the institution conferring the degree.

Sec. 7.—No secondary school shall be eligible to membership which does not have a four years' course of study.

ARTICLE IV.

POWERS.

All the decisions of the Association bearing upon the policy and management of higher and secondary institutions are understood to be advisory in their character.

ARTICLE V.

OFFICERS AND COMMITTEES.

Section 1.—The officers of the Association shall be a President, two Vice-Presidents from each state represented in the Association, a Secretary, a Treasurer, and an Executive Committee consisting of the President, the Secretary, the Treasurer, and four other members elected by the Association.

Sec. 2.—The officers shall be chosen at the annual meeting for the term of one year, or until their successors are elected. The election shall be by ballot.

Sec. 3.—The Executive Committee shall have power to appoint committees for conference with other bodies, whenever in their judgment it may seem expedient.

Sec. 4.—In case an officer holding office as representative of an institutional member severs his connection with the institution represented, he shall at his discretion hold his office until the close of the next regular meeting of the Association.

Sec. 5.—The Executive Committee shall have authority to fill a vacancy in any office, the officer elected by the committee to hold office until the close of the next annual meeting.

ARTICLE VI.

DUTIES OF OFFICERS.

Section 1.—The President, or in his absence one of the Vice-Presidents selected by the Executive Committee, shall preside at the meetings of the Association, and shall sign all orders upon the Treasurer.

Sec. 2.—The Secretary shall keep a record of the proceedings of the Association and attend to all necessary correspondence and printing.

Sec. 3.—The Treasurer shall collect and hold all moneys of the Association, and pay out the same upon the written order of the President.

Sec. 4.—The Executive Committee shall make all nominations for membership in the Association, fix the time of all meetings not otherwise provided for, prepare programmes, and act for the Association when it is not in session. All the acts of the Executive Committee shall be subject to the approval of the Association.

ARTICLE VII.

MEETINGS.

There shall be an annual meeting of the Association and such special meetings as the Association may appoint.

ARTICLE VIII.

MEMBERSHIP FEE.

To meet expenses, an annual fee of $3.00 shall be paid by each member, and each member shall have one vote.

ARTICLE IX.

QUORUM.

One-fourth of the members of the Association shall constitute a quorum.

ARTICLE X.

AMENDMENTS.

This constitution may be amended by a three-fourths vote at any regular meeting, provided that a printed notice of the proposed amendment be sent to each member two weeks before said meeting.

OFFICERS FOR THE YEAR 1902-1903.

PRESIDENT.

George N. Carman, Director of Lewis Institute, Chicago, Ill.

VICE-PRESIDENTS.

Ohio.

Chas. F. Thwing, President of Western Reserve University, Cleveland.

E. W. Coy, Principal of Hughes High School, Cincinnati.

Michigan.

Francis W. Kelsey, Professor in the University of Michigan, Ann Arbor.

F. L. Bliss, Principal of the Detroit University School, Detroit.

Indiana.

Joseph Swain, President of the University of Indiana, Bloomington.

Edward Ayres, Superintendent, Lafayette.

Illinois.

W. R. Harper, President of the University of Chicago, Chicago.

A. F. Nightingale, Superintendent of Schools of Cook County, Chicago.

Wisconsin.

E. A. Birge, Professor in the University of Wisconsin, Madison.

A. W. Tressler, Inspector of High Schools, Madison.

Minnesota.

W. N. West, Professor in the University of Minnesota, Minneapolis.

F. A. Weld, President of the Moorhead Normal School, Moorhead.

Iowa.

Wm. F. King, President of Cornell College, Mt. Vernon.

H. H. Seerley, President of the State Normal School, Cedar Falls.

Missouri.

M. S. Snow, Professor in the Washington University, St. Louis.

W. J. S. Bryan, Principal of the High School, St. Louis.

Nebraska.

E. B. Andrews, President of the University of Nebraska, Lincoln.

H. J. Davenport, Principal of the High School, Lincoln.

Kansas.

F. H. Snow, Professor in the University of Kansas, Lawrence.

W. A. Davidson, Superintendent, Topeka.

Colorado.

J. H. Baker, President of the University of Colorado.

W. H. Smiley, Principal of High School No. 1, Denver.

SECRETARY.

F. N. Scott, Professor in the University of Michigan, Ann Arbor.

TREASURER.

Jas. E. Armstrong, Principal of Englewood High School, Chicago.

EXECUTIVE COMMITTEE.

The President, Secretary, Treasurer, and

C. A. Waldo, Professor in Purdue University, Lafayette, Indiana.

E. L. Harris, Principal of the Central High School, Cleveland, Ohio.

J. R. Kirk, President of the State Normal School, Kirksville, Missouri.

G. E. MacLean, President of the University of Iowa, Iowa City.

REGISTRATION.

Albright, C. E. Central High School, Columbus, Ohio.

Allen, Dudley P., Professor. Western Reserve University, Cleveland, Ohio.

Anderson, H. S. University School, Cleveland, Ohio.

Armstrong, J. E., Principal. Englewood High School, Chicago.

Ayres, Edw., Superintendent. Lafayette, Indiana.

Baker, J. H., President. University of Colorado, Boulder, Colorado.

Ballou, C. G., Principal. Central High School, Toledo, Ohio.

Barrett, Chas. S. South High School, Columbus, Ohio.

Barrows, J. H., President. Oberlin College, Oberlin, Ohio.

Bedgood, R. K. High School, Lafayette, Indiana.

Bell, Miss Daisy. High School, Wellington, Ohio.

Beman, W. W., Professor. University of Michigan, Ann Arbor, Michigan.

Benjamin, Chas. H. Case School of Applied Science, Cleveland, Ohio.

Bill, Clarence P. Adelbert College, Cleveland, Ohio.

Black, W. H., President. Missouri Valley College, Marshall, Missouri.

Bliss, F. L. Detroit University School, Detroit, Michigan.

Bridgman, W. R. Lake Forest University, Lake Forest, Illinois.

Brown, Abram. East High School, Columbus, Ohio.

Brown, J. F. State University of Iowa, Iowa City.

Bryan, W. J. S., Principal. Normal and High School, St. Louis, Missouri.

Bryan, Mrs. W. J. S. St. Louis, Missouri.

Carman, Geo. N., Director. Lewis Institute, Chicago.

Coy, E. W., Principal. Hughes High School, Cincinnati, Ohio.

Curtis, M. W. Western Reserve University, Cleveland, Ohio.

Dean, E. P. High School, Ashland, Ohio.

Denney, Joseph V., Professor. Ohio State University, Columbus, Ohio.

Dickerman, John. Adelbert College. Cleveland. Ohio.

Dougherty, N. C., Superintendent. Peoria, Illinois.

Draper, A. S., President. University of Illinois, Urbana, Illinois.

Eagleson, S. 691 East Prospect St., Cleveland, Ohio.

Ebert, H. M. High School, Elyria, Ohio.

Everett, Chas. D. North High School, Columbus, Ohio.

Fife, Robert H., Jr. Adelbert College, Cleveland, Ohio.

Foote, Alice M. High School, Oberlin, Ohio.

Foote, Eunice S. Oberlin, Ohio.

Frederick, J. M. H. High School, Lakewood, Ohio.

French, C. H. 84 Arlington St., Cleveland, Ohio.

Garbutt, I. R. Central High School, Cleveland, Ohio.

Gilpatrick, J. L. Denison University, Granville, Ohio.

Graber, Philip E. High School, Akron, Ohio.

Grant, U. S. Northwestern University, Evanston, Ill.

Griffin, L E. Western Reserve University, Cleveland, Ohio.

Griswold, Wells L. Rayen High School, Youngstown, Ohio.

Harlan, Richard D., President. Lake Forest University, Lake Forest, Illinois.

Harris, Edward L., Principal. Central High School, Cleveland, Ohio.

Hartwell, S. O., Superintendent. Kalamazoo, Michigan.

Hickok, Chas. T. Western Reserve Academy, Hudson, Ohio.

Hieronymus, Robert E., President. Eureka College, Eureka, Illinois.

Hitchcock, Miss C. M. Lake Erie College, Painesville, Ohio.

Hobbie, Jas. G. Central Institute, Cleveland, Ohio.

Hood, Albert C. Central High School, Cleveland, Ohio.

Howe, Chas. S. Case School of Applied Science, Cleveland, Ohio.

Johnson, G. E. University School, Cleveland, Ohio.

Johnson, J. S., Superintendent. Salem, Ohio.

Johnston, Theo. H., Principal. West High School, Cleveland, Ohio.

Jones, Franklin I. South High School, Cleveland, Ohio.

Jones, George N. Oberlin College, Oberlin, Ohio.

Judson, Harry Pratt, Dean. University of Chicago, Chicago, Illinois.

King, H. C., Professor. Oberlin College, Oberlin, Ohio.

Kirk, John R., President. Kirksville Normal School, Kirksville, Missouri.

Knight, Chas. M. Buchtel College, Akron, Ohio.

La Shell, Lewis L. Case School of Applied Science, Cleveland, Ohio.

Lehman, D. A. Adelbert College, Cleveland, Ohio.

Lewis, M. F. High School, Geneva, Ohio.

Locke, Geo. Herbert. University of Chicago, Chicago, Illinois.

Loomis, Elisha S. West High School, Cleveland, Ohio.

McAfee, Lowell M., President. Park College, Parkville, Missouri.

McCollum, H. B. Geneva, Ohio.

MacCracken, John H., President. Westminster College, Fulton, Missouri.

McKean, T. L. West High School, Cleveland, Ohio.

Maynard, Miss Vivian H. Glenville, Ohio.

Miller, E. A. High School, Oberlin, Ohio.

Mooney, Granville W. Grand River Institute, Austinburg, Ohio.

Morton, H. N. High School, Sandusky, Ohio.

Nightingale, A. F. 1997 Sheridan Road, Chicago, Ill.

Olin, Oscar E., Principal. Buchtel Academy, Akron, O.

Oliver, T. E. Western Reserve University, Cleveland, Ohio.

Parkhurst, C. P. Columbus, Ohio.

Pearson, F. B. East High School, Columbus, Ohio.

Perrin, John W. Western Reserve University, Cleveland, Ohio.

Phypers, Mrs. G. W. 83 Knowles St., East Cleveland, O.

Rankin, Homes D. High School, Euclid, Ohio.

Rice, Edw. L. Ohio Wesleyan University, Delaware, O.

Rogers, Geo. E., Superintendent. Jefferson Educational Institute, Jefferson, Ohio.

Rybolt, D. C., Principal. High School, Akron, Ohio.

St. John, C. E., Professor. Oberlin College, Oberlin, O.

Scott, F. N., Professor. University of Michigan, Ann Arbor, Michigan.

Shauer, J. C. Lake Forest Academy, Lake Forest, Ill.

Shaw, John T. Oberlin Academy, Oberlin, Ohio.

Sheffield, A. D. University School, Cleveland, Ohio.

Sluss, H. O. Western Reserve Academy, Hudson, Ohio.

Smiley, Jas. B. Lincoln High School, Cleveland, Ohio.

Smith, Chas. J. Western Reserve University, Cleveland, Ohio.

Snow, Marshall S. Washington University, St. Louis, Missouri.

Spanton, A. I. Buchtel Academy, Akron, Ohio.

Staley, Cady, President. Case School of Applied Science, Cleveland, Ohio.

Stevens, C. E. South High School, Cleveland, Ohio.

Stewart, N. Coe. Rose Building, Cleveland, Ohio.

Streich, Albert C. Central High School, Cleveland, Ohio.

Swain, Joseph, President. University of Indiana, Bloomington, Indiana.

Thwing, Chas. F., President. Western Reserve University, Cleveland, Ohio.

Thorndike, A. H. Western Reserve University, Cleveland, Ohio.

Tower, O. F. Adelbert College, Cleveland, Ohio.

Treudley, F. Youngstown, Ohio.

Turner, A. E., President. Waynesburg College, Waynesburg, Pennsylvania.

Twiss, George R. Central High School, Cleveland, Ohio.

Upton, Ralph R. High School, Chillicothe, Ohio.

Van Horn, Frank R. Case School of Applied Science, Cleveland, Ohio.

Waldo, C. A., Professor. Purdue University, Lafayette, Indiana.

Ward, T. D. Lorain, Ohio.

Webster, Mary S. High School, Geneva, Ohio.

Whitman, Frank P. Adelbert College, Cleveland, Ohio.

Whitney, A. S., Professor. University of Michigan, Ann Arbor, Michigan.

Whitney, Frank P. High School, Collinwood, Ohio.

Williams, H. B. High School, Sandusky, Ohio.

Wolcott, Emil P. High School, Akron, Ohio.

Wood, Herbert C. East High School, Cleveland, Ohio.

Woodward, C. M., Professor. Washington University, St. Louis, Missouri.

Wright, A. S. Case School of Applied Science, Cleveland, Ohio.

APPENDIX TO THE PROCEEDINGS OF THE SEVENTH
ANNUAL MEETING OF THE ASSOCIATION OF COLLEGES AND
SECONDARY SCHOOLS OF THE NORTH CENTRAL STATES

1902

REPORT

OF THE

COMMISSION ON ACCREDITED

SCHOOLS

PUBLISHED BY THE ASSOCIATION
1902

NOTICE.

The following pages form part of the Proceedings of the Seventh Annual Meeting of the North Central Association of Colleges and Secondary Schools. The price of this volume of the Proceedings entire is twenty-five cents. The price of the Appendix, printed separately, is ten cents. Copies of either may be obtained by addressing the Treasurer of the Association, Principal J. E. Armstrong, Englewood High School, Chicago.

ORGANIZATION OF THE COMMISSION.

At the sixth annual meeting of the North Central Association of Colleges and Secondary Schools, a paper was read by Dean S. A. Forbes, of the University of Illinois, on "The Desirability of so Federating the North Central Colleges and Universities as to Secure Essentially Uniform or at Least Equivalent Entrance Requirements."[1]

As the outcome of the paper and the discussion which followed it, a committee consisting of Dean S. A. Forbes, of the University of Illinois (chairman); President Cady Staley, of the Case School of Applied Science; President W. R. Harper, of the University of Chicago; Principal C. G. Ballou, of the Toledo High School; and Professor Stanley Coulter, of Purdue University, was appointed by the Association, March 29, 1901, to take into consideration and to report, on the following day, some plan of action embodying the idea outlined by Dean Forbes and the suggestions thrown out in the course of the discussion of the paper.

The report of the committee was as follows:

To the North Central Association of Colleges and Secondary Schools:

Your committee has considered the subject assigned to it as carefully as the brief time at our disposal would permit and under a sense of responsibility, we hope, corresponding to the importance of the subject. We have not

---

[1] Printed in full in the Proceedings of the Sixth Annual Meeting of the North Central Association of Colleges and Secondary Schools, pp. 11–21.

attempted to reach conclusions, or even to raise questions, on any of the issues involved in the establishment of fixed and uniform relations between the colleges and secondary schools, but have thought it best to leave the whole matter, subject to the instructions of the Association, to a permanent commission, whose appointment we recommend. This Commission we have sought to make thoroughly representative, thoroughly responsible and practically efficient; and we believe that, if constituted in some such form as proposed, and inspired by the colleges with a determination to reach tangible results without delay, it will prove to be a very influential and important agency of educational progress. The propositions of the committee are presented in the following recommendation:

We recommend that the Association do now proceed to the establishment of some definite form of affiliation and credit, as fixed, comprehensive, and uniform as may be, between the colleges and universities of this Association and the secondary schools of the North Central states, and to this end we make the following recommendations:

(1) That a permanent commission be formed to be called the *Commission on Accredited Schools* and to consist, first, of twelve members to be appointed by the Chair, six from the colleges and six representing the secondary schools; and second, of additional or delegate members one from each college or university belonging to the Association which has a freshman class of at least fifty members and which may appoint such a representative, together with a sufficient number of members from the secondary schools, to be appointed by the Chair, to maintain a parity of representation as between the secondary schools and the colleges. The term of service of the twelve members of the first class should be three years, two college representatives and two representatives of the secondary schools to be now appointed for one year, two

of each for two years, and two of each for three years; and vacancies to be filled in the same manner as the original appointments are made. The appointment of additional high school members should be for one year, subject, of course, to renewal by the appointing officer. We suggest that the President of this Association serve as temporary chairman of this Commission until it has met and organized by the selection of its own officers.

(2) That it be made the duty of this Commission to define and describe unit courses of study in the various subjects of the high school programme, taking for the point of departure the recommendations of the National Committee of Thirteen; to serve as a standing committee on uniformity of admission requirements for the colleges and universities of this Association; to take steps to secure uniformity in the standards and methods, and economy of labor and expense, in the work of high school inspection; to prepare a list of high schools within the territory of this Association which are entitled to the accredited relationship; and to formulate and report methods and standards for the assignment of college credit for good high school work done in advance of the college entrance requirement.

(3) We recommend that the expenses necessarily attendant upon the work of this Commission be assumed by the colleges represented on it in proportion to membership in their freshman classes.

The committee assumes that this Commission would usually hold at least annual meetings immediately preceding those of the Association itself, and in time to report its action to the Association for approval.

After considerable discussion the report was adopted without change. The president appointed the following persons as members of the Commission on Accredited Schools:

For one year: President E. B. Andrews, of the University of Nebraska; President G. E. MacLean, of the University of Iowa; President John R. Kirk, of the Missouri State Normal School, Kirksville; Director G. N. Carman, of the Lewis Institute, Chicago.

For two years: Dean Harry Pratt Judson, of the University of Chicago; Professor Stanley Coulter, of Purdue University; Superintendent A. F. Nightingale, of Chicago; Superintendent C. N. Kendall, of Indianapolis.

For three years: Dean E. A. Birge, of the University of Wisconsin; President James H. Baker, of the University of Colorado; Inspector A. S. Whitney, of the University of Michigan; Principal E. L. Harris, of Cleveland.

The Commission organized March 30, 1901, the following members being present: Messrs. MacLean, Baker, Harris, Whitney, Coulter, Kirk, and Carman.

Professor Judson was elected chairman of the Commission, and Director Carman, secretary. It was voted, (1) that a meeting of the Commission be held in Chicago in February, at the time of the meeting of the Department of Superintendence of the National Educational Association, (2) that the chairman delegate to the members of the Commission such duties as he may see fit, and (3) that the colleges of the Association be requested to appoint delegate members of the Commission not later than Dec. 15, 1901.

The second meeting of the Commission was held in Chicago, Feb. 25, 1902. There was a general discussion of plans, and it was agreed that four committees be appointed by the Chair. These committees were as follows:

1. Executive Committee: The Chairman and the Secretary of the Commission; Professor Coulter, of Purdue University; Principal Coy, of Cincinnati; and Superintendent Kendall, of Indianapolis.

2. Committee on Unit Courses of Study: Principal Bliss, of Detroit University School; Professor King, of Oberlin College; Professor Birge, of the University of Wisconsin; Principal French, of Hyde Park High School; and Director Carman, of Lewis Institute.

3. Committee on High School Inspection: Inspector Whitney, of Michigan; Inspector Aiton, of Minnesota; Inspector Tressler, of Wisconsin; Inspector Brown, of Iowa; and President Kirk, of Missouri.

4. Committee on College Credit for High School Work: Professor Denney, of Ohio State University; Professor Snow, of Washington University; Professor Vincent, of the University of Chicago; Principal Lane, of Fort Wayne High School; and Superintendent Nightingale, of Chicago.

After deciding upon plans of work for the several committees, the Commission adjourned to meet in Cleveland, March 27, 1902.

The third meeting of the Commission was held in Cleveland on the 27th of March, 1902. The committees reported in full, and their reports were exhaustively discussed, amended and adopted by the Commission.

The Commission presented its first annual report to the Association on March 28. After discussion and amendment it was adopted by the Association as herein presented, the reports of the sub-committees on Unit Courses of Study and on College Credit for High School Work being incorporated in it. The report of the sub-committee on High School Inspection, though it forms part of the Report of the Commission, is appended as a separate document.

REPORT OF THE COMMISSION ON ACCREDITED SCHOOLS.

UNIT COURSES IN GENERAL.

1. A unit course of study is defined as a course covering a school year of not less than thirty-five weeks, with four or five periods of at least forty-five minutes each per week.

2. The graduation requirement of the high school and the entrance requirement of the college shall include fifteen units as above defined.

3. All high school curricula and all requirements for college entrance shall include as constants three units of English and two units of mathematics.

COLLEGE CREDIT FOR WORK DONE IN SECONDARY SCHOOLS.

1. The Commission favors the general principle that colleges should give advanced credit for secondary school work, when sufficient in amount and quality, done in addition to the fifteen units required for admission.

2. In the opinion of the Commission no advanced college credit should be given for less than one full year of secondary school work in any subject, except so far as half units are specified in the definitions of unit courses, or for any study that is not pursued later than the second year of the high school course.

3. The amount of advanced credit to be awarded in any subject should be determined by the college which the student enters.

UNIT COURSES IN PARTICULAR SUBJECTS.

English (3 units).

The three units in English should cover the following subjects:

(a) *Grammar.* The student should have a sufficient

knowledge of English grammar to enable him at need to point out the syntactical structure of any sentence which he encounters in the prescribed reading. He should also be able to state intelligently the leading grammatical principles when he is called upon to do so. Whether this knowledge is obtained in the elementary school and the secondary school combined or only in the elementary school is immaterial, provided the student have it; but in most cases it cannot be acquired except through regular study and practice in the lower grades and occasional reviews in the higher, and scarce through these. A progressive and regular development of the grammar-sense from the lowest grades to the highest is much to be preferred to a sudden and unprepared-for injection of formal grammar at a particular stage, as, for example, in the eighth grade.

(b) *Reading.* The books prescribed by the Joint Committee on Uniform Entrance Requirements in English form the basis for this part of the work. It is expected that all students shall read these books intelligently and appreciatively, but it is important to understand that the list is prescribed neither as a maximum nor as a minimum requirement. Rather these books are intended to serve as a common center from which each school shall proceed with such wider courses of English study as it may find profitable. It is taken for granted that each school will arrange for a considerable amount of outside reading supplementary to the prescribed readings.

The list, as arranged by the Joint Committee on Entrance Requirements in English, is divided into two parts, the first consisting of books to be read with attention to their contents rather than to their form, the second consisting of books to be studied thoroughly and minutely. The lists, thus divided, are as follows:

I. BOOKS PRESCRIBED FOR READING.

For 1903, 1904, and 1905: Shakespeare's *The Merchant of Venice* and *Julius Caesar;* The *Sir Roger De Coverley Papers* in the Spectator; Goldsmith's *The Vicar of Wakefield;* Coleridge's *The Ancient Mariner;* Scott's *Ivanhoe;* Carlyle's *Essay on Burns;* Tennyson's *The Princess;* Lowell's *The Vision of Sir Launfal;* George Eliot's *Silas Marner.*

For 1906, 1907, and 1908: Shakespeare's *The Merchant of Venice and Macbeth;* The Sir Roger de Coverley Papers in *The Spectator;* Irving's *Life of Goldsmith;* Coleridge's *The Ancient Mariner;* Scott's *Ivanhoe* and *The Lady of the Lake;* Tennyson's *Gareth and Lynette, Lancelot and Elaine,* and *The Passing of Arthur;* Lowell's *The Vision of Sir Launfal;* Georgie Eliot's *Silas Marner.*

II. BOOKS PRESCRIBED FOR STUDY AND PRACTICE.

For 1903, 1904, and 1905: Shakespeare's *Macbeth;* Milton's *Lycidas, Comus, L'Allegro, and Il Penseroso;* Burke's *Speech on Conciliation with America;* Macaulay's *Essays on Milton and Addison.*

For 1906, 1907, and 1908: Shakespeare's *Julius Caesar;* Milton's *Lycidas, Comus, L'Allegro and Il Penseroso;* Burke's *Speech on Conciliation with America;* Macaulay's *Essay on Addison* and *Life of Johnson.*

With reference to the second list, the Joint Committee recommends that each of the books prescribed for study be taught with reference to subject matter, form and structure; and that, in addition, attention be given to the essentials of English grammar and to the leading facts in those periods of English literary history to which the prescribed works belong.

The above lists and requirements are intended to indicate in a general way the extent and character of the required work, and are not to be interpreted as limitations upon the teacher's choice. Books of equal merit, covering a similar range of literary types, will meet the requirements satisfactorily.

(c) *Composition.* Regular and persistent training in both written and oral composition should be given throughout the entire school course. In the high school, instruction in this subject should not be broken up into term or semester courses, but should be regarded as continuous throughout the four years. As regards the subjects for composition, they should be taken in the high school course partly from the list of books prescribed for study and practice, or from other literature which the class may read; partly from the student's own thought and experience. The topics should be so chosen as to give practice in the four leading types of prose discourse, namely, Description, Narration, Exposition and Argument.

(d) *Rhetoric.* It is expected that the student will be familiar with the essential principles of rhetoric. The instruction in this subject should begin early in the high school course in connection with the work in composition, and should include the following particulars: choice of words; structure of sentences and paragraphs; the principles of narration, description, exposition and argument. The teacher should distinguish between those parts of rhetorical theory which are retained in text-books merely through the influence of tradition and those which have direct bearing upon the composition work. The former may be safely omitted.

Mathematics (4 units).

In mathematics the commission adopts the statement of the College Entrance Examination Board, except that a somewhat smaller portion in algebra is assigned to the first year, and a review of essentials is recommended in connection with the advanced course in algebra.

1. *Algebra.* The four fundamental operations for rational algebraic expressions, factoring, highest common factor, lowest common multiple, complex fractions, the solution of equations of the first degree containing one or more unknown quantities, radicals, including the extraction of the square root of polynomials and numbers, and fractional and negative exponents. Quadratic equations and equations containing one or more unknown quantities that can be solved by the methods of quadratic equations, problems depending upon such equations.

2. *Plane Geometry,* including the solution of simple original exercises and numerical problems.

3a. *Algebra.* A review of the essentials to be followed by ratio and proportion, and the binomial theorem for positive integral exponents. The progressions, the elementary treatment of permutations and combinations, and the use of four and five place tables of logarithms.

3b. *Solid Geometry,* including properties of straight lines and planes, of dihedral and polyhedral angles, of projections, of polyhedrons, including prisms, pyramids and the regular solids, of cylinders, cones and spheres, of spherical triangles, and the measurement of surfaces and solids.

4a. *Algebra.* Undetermined coefficients, the elementary treatment of infinite series, the binomial theorem for fractional and negative exponents, and the theory of logarithms.

Determinants, and the elements of the theory of equations, including Horner's method for solving numerical equations.

4b. *Trigonometry.* Plane Trigonometry, including the definitions and relations of the six trigonometrical functions as ratios, proof of important formulæ, theory of logarithms and use of tables, solution of right and oblique plane triangles. Spherical Trigonometry, including the proof of important formulæ and the solution of right and oblique spherical triangles with the proper interpretation of the ambiguous cases.

History (4 units).

1. Ancient history, with special reference to Greek and Roman history, and including also a short introductory study of the more ancient nations and the chief events of the early middle ages, down to the death of Charlemagne (814).

2. Mediæval and modern European history, from the death of Charlemagne to the present time.

3. English history.

4. American history, or American history and civil government.

The periods that are here indicated as constituting the four units were recommended by the Committee of Seven of the American Historical Association in their report to the Association in 1899. The full report is published under the title "The Study of History in Schools." It contains suggestions as to various methods of treating these periods, and gives further information likely to be of service to the teacher. A short course of one year in general history of the world has been in a great measure abandoned by the schools, because it does not give the opportunity for the more concrete study and for the training in historical thinking that can be obtained from the more intensive work. The plan of continuing ancient history to the time of Charlemagne or the establishment of the Holy Roman Empire has much to commend it, and is now adopted in many schools. Excellent books have been prepared which will enable the teachers to cover the field, as a whole, satisfactorily. By continuing the study of ancient history down into the early middle ages, a reasonable adjustment of time between the earlier and later periods is secured; and from the purely historical as well as the pedagogical point of view, there is much to be said in favor of connecting Roman history with the later times; the pupil is not left in the confusion of the fallen or the decadent empire. In connection with a year's work in American history much instruction can be given in civil government; a course dwelling on the development of American political ideals and the actual workings of institutions necessarily gives information concretely of the present governmental forms and methods.

No definite statement need be made concerning the mode of teaching or the apparatus that should be used. But it may be said that the mere learning of a text will not give the preparation that the colleges desire. Happily the time is gone when teachers are inclined to confine their classes to the memorizing of a single text. Some colleges in their entrance examination expect the candidate to present note-books showing the amount and character of the work done in the schools. It is desirable that note-books or cards should be kept as a record of the work done. They may contain copious extracts from primary and secondary authorities, references to important material, sketch maps made by the pupils as illustrations of their studies, and informal notes on reading that has been done in connection with the course. Such work is necessary if the historical courses are to give their best educational results. Effort should be made to cultivate the power of handling facts and of drawing proper inductions from data, to develop the faculty of discrimination, to teach the pupils the use of books and how to extract substance from the printed page. The acquisition of information alone can not be the chief aim of any school work; knowledge of how to acquire information and, above all, some skill in putting forth what one knows must always be of more than secondary importance; history therefore should be taught as a disciplinary and educational subject.

Latin (4 units).

In Latin the commission adopts the first two units as defined by the American Philological Association, and the third and fourth units as defined by the College Entrance Examination Board.

1. Latin lessons, accompanied from an early stage by the reading of very simple selections. Easy reading: twenty to thirty pages of consecutive text.

In all written exercises the long vowels should be marked, and in all oral exercises pains should be taken to make the pronunciation conform to the quantities.

The student should be trained from the beginning to grasp the meaning of the Latin before translating, and then to render into idiomatic English; and should be taught to read the Latin aloud with intelligent expression.

2. Selections from Cæsar's Gallic War equivalent in amount to four books; selections from other prose writers, such as Nepos, may be taken as a substitute for an amount up to, but not exceeding, two books.

The equivalent of at least one period a week in prose composition based on Cæsar.

Reading aloud and translating, together with training in correct methods of apprehending the author's meaning, both prepared and unprepared passages being used as material. The memorizing of selected passages.

3, 4. Cicero: Any six orations from the following list, but preferably the first six mentioned:

The four orations against Catiline, Archias, the Manilian Law, Marcellus, Roscius, Milo, Sestius, Ligarius, the fourteenth Philippic.

Vergil: The first six books of the Aeneid.

The equivalent of at least one period a week in prose composition based on Cicero.

Note: In place of a part of Cicero an equivalent of Sallust's Catiline, and in place of a part of Vergil an equivalent of Ovid will be accepted.

Greek (3 units).

In Greek the definitions of the three units of the Philological Association are adopted.

1. Introductory lessons:
    Xenophon's Anabasis (20 to 30 pages).
    Practice in reading at sight and in writing Greek.
    Systematic study of grammar begun.

2. Xenophon's Anabasis (continued), either alone or with other Attic prose (75 to 120 pages).

Practice in reading at sight, systematic study of grammar, thorough grammatical review, and practice in writing Greek, both based on study of Books I and II of the Anabasis.

3. Homer (2,500 to 4,000 lines); e. g., Iliad, I-III (omitting II, 494-end), and VI-VIII.

Attic prose (33 to 40 pages), with practice in writing Greek; grammar; practice reading at sight.

French (4 units).

The definitions of the four units in French and the four units in German are those recommended by the Committee of Twelve of the Modern Language Association.

1. During the first year the work should comprise: (1) careful drill in pronunciation; (2) the rudiments of grammar, including the inflection of the regular and the more common irregular verbs, the plural of nouns, the inflection of adjectives, participles, and pronouns; the use of personal pronouns, common adverbs, prepositions, and conjunctions; the order of words in the sentence, and the elementary rules of syntax; (3) abundant easy exercises, designed not only to fix in the memory the forms and principles of grammar, but also to cultivate readiness in the reproduction of natural forms of expression; (4)

the reading of from 100 to 175 duodecimo pages of graduated texts, with constant practice in translating into
French easy variations of the sentences read (the teacher
giving the English), and in reproducing from memory
sentences previously read; (5) writing French from
dictation.

2. During the second year the work should comprise:
(1) the reading of from 250 to 400 pages of easy modern
prose in the form of stories, plays, or historical or bio-
graphical sketches; (2) constant practice, as in the pre-
vious year, in translating into French easy variations upon
the texts read; (3) frequent abstracts, sometimes oral and
sometimes written, of portions of the text already read;
(4) writing French from dictation; (5) continued drill
upon the rudiments of grammar, with constant application
in the construction of sentences; (6) mastery of the forms
and use of pronouns, pronominal adjectives, of all but the
rare irregular verb forms, and of the simpler uses of the
conditional and subjunctive.

Suitable texts for the second year are: About's *Le
roi des montagnes,* Bruno's *Le tour de la France,* Daudet's
easier short tales, La Bedolliere's *La Mère Michel et son
chat,* Erckmann-Chatrian's stories, Foa's *Contes bio-
graphiques* and *Le Petit Robinson de Paris,* Fon-
cin's *Le pays de France,* Labiche and Martin's *La poudre
aux yeux* and *Le voyage de M. Perrichon,* Legouvé and
Labiche's *La cigale chez les fourmis,* Malot's *Sans fami-
lle,* Mairet's *La tache du petit Pierre,* Merimee's *Colomba,*
extracts from Michelet, Sarcey's *Le siége de Paris,*
Verne's stories.

3. This should comprise the reading of from 400 to
600 pages of French of ordinary difficulty. a portion to be
in the dramatic form; constant practice in giving French
paraphrases, abstracts or reproductions from memory of
selected portions of the matter read; the study of a grammar of moderate completeness; writing from dictation.

Suitable texts are: About's stories, Augier and Sandeau's *Le Gendre de M. Poirier,* Beranger's poems, Corneille's *Le Cid* and *Horace,* Coppee's poems. Daudet's *La
Belle-Nivernaise,* La Brète's *Mon oncle et mon curé,* Mad-
ame de Sévigné's letters, Hugo's *Hernani* and *La chute,*
Labiche's plays, Loti's *Pêcheur d'Islande,* Mignet's historical writings, Moliere's *L'avare* and *Le Bourgeois Gen-
tilhomme,* Racine's *Athalie, Andromaque,* and *Esther,*
George Sand's plays and stories, Sandeau's *Mademoiselle
de la Seiglière,* Scribe's plays, Thierry's *Récits des temps
mérovingiens.* Thiers' *L'expédition de Bonaparte en
Egypte.* Vigny's *La canne de jonc,* Voltaire's historical
writings.

4. This should comprise the reading of from 600 to
1,000 pages of standard French, classical and modern,
only difficult passages being explained in the class; the
writing of numerous short themes in French; the study
of syntax. One unit.

Suitable reading matter will be: Beaumarchias's *Bar-
bier de Seville;* Corneille's dramas; the elder Dumas's
prose writings; the younger Dumas's *La question d'ar-
gent;* Hugo's *Ruy Blas,* lyrics and prose writings; La
Fontaine's fables; Lamartine's *Graziella;* Marivaux's
plays; Moliere's plays; Musset's plays and poems; Pellis-
sier's *Mouvement littéraire au XIXᵉ siècle;* Renan's
Souvenirs d'enfance et de jeunesse; Rousseau's writings;
Sainte-Beuve's essays; Taine's *Origines de la France con-
temporaine;* Voltaire's writings; selections from Zola,
Maupassant, and Balzac.

German (4 units.)

1. During the first year the work should comprise:
(1) careful drill upon pronunciation; (2) the memorizing
and frequent repetition of easy colloquial sentences; (3)
drill upon the rudiments of grammar, that is, upon the
inflection of the articles, of such nouns as belong to the

language of everyday life, of adjectives, pronouns, weak verbs, and the more usual strong verbs; also upon the use of the more common prepositions, the simpler uses of the modal auxiliaries, and the elementary rules of syntax and word-order; (4) abundant easy exercises designed not only to fix in mind the forms and principles of grammar, but also to cultivate readiness in the reproduction of natural forms of expression: (5) the reading of from 75 to 100 pages of graduated texts from a reader, with constant practice in translating into German easy variations upon sentences selected from the reading lesson (the teacher giving the English), and in the reproduction from memory of sentences previously read.

2. During the second year the work should comprise: (1) the reading of from 150 to 200 pages of literature in the form of easy stories and plays: (2) accompanying practice, as before, in the translation into German of easy variations upon the matter read, and also in the off-hand reproduction, sometimes orally and sometimes in writing, of the substance of short and easy selected passages; (3) continued drill upon the rudiments of the grammar, directed to the ends of enabling the pupil, first. to use his knowledge with facility in the formation of sentences, and, secondly, to state his knowledge correctly in the technical language of grammar.

Stories suitable for the elementary course can be selected from the following list: Andersen's *Maerchen* and *Bilderbuch ohne Bilder;* Arnold's *Fritz auf Ferien;* Baumbach's *Die Nonna* and *Der Schwiegersohn;* Gerstaecker's *Germelshausen;* Heyse's *L'Arrabbiata, Das Maedchen von Treppi,* and *Anfang und Ende;* Hillern's *Hoeher als die Kirche;* Jensen's *Die braune Erica;* Leander's *Traeumereien,* and *Kleine Geshichten;* Seidel's *Maerchen;* Stoekl's *Unter dem Christbaum;* Storm's *Immensee* and *Geschichten aus der Tonne;* Zschokke's *Der zerbrochene Krug.*

Good plays adapted to the elementary course are much harder to find than good stories. Five-act plays are too long. They require more time than it is advisable to devote to any one text. Among shorter plays the best available are perhaps Benedix's *Der Prozess, Der Weiberfeind,* and *Guenstige Vorzeichen;* Elz's *Er ist nicht eifersuechtig;* Wichert's *An der Majorsecke;* Wilhelmi's *Einer muss heiraten.* It is recommended, however, that not more than one of these plays be read. The narrative style should predominate. A good selection of reading matter for the second year would be Andersen's *Maerchen,* or *Bilderbuch,* or Leander's *Traeumereien,* to the extent of, say, forty pages. After that such a story as *Das kalte Herz;* or, *Der zerbrochene Krug;* then *Hoeher als die Kirche,* or *Immensee;* next a good story by Heyse, Baumbach, or Seidel: lastly *Der Prozess.*

3. The work should comprise, in addition to the elementary course, the reading of about 400 pages of moderately difficult prose and poetry, with constant practice in giving, sometimes orally and sometimes in writing, paraphrases, abstracts, or reproductions from memory of selected portions of the matter read; also grammatical drill upon the less usual strong verbs, the use of articles, cases, auxiliaries of all kinds, tenses and modes (with special reference to the infinitive and subjunctive), and likewise upon word-order and word-formation.

Suitable reading for the third year can be selected from such works as the following: Ebner-Eschenbach's *Die Freiherren von Gemperlein;* Freytag's *Die Journalisten* and *Bilder aus der deutschen Vergangenheit*—for example *Karl der Grosse, Aus den Kreuzzuegen, Doktor Luther, Aus dem Staat Friedrich's des Grossen;* Fouqué's *Undine;* Gerstaecker's *Irrefahrten;* Goethe's *Hermann und Dorothea* and *Iphigenie;* Heine's poems and *Reisebilder;* Hoffmann's *Historische Erzaehlungen;* Lessing's *Minna von Barnhelm;* Meyer's *Gustav Adolf's Page;* Moser's

Der Bibliothekar; Riehl's *Novellen*—for example, *Burg Neideck,Der Fluch der Schoenheit,Der stumme Ratsherr, Das Spielmannkind;* Rosegger's *Waldheimat;* Schiller's *Der Neffe als Onkel, Der Geisterseher, Wilhelm Tell, Die Jungfrau von Orleans, Das lied von der Glocke, Balladen;* Scheffel's *Der Trompeter von Saekkingen;* Uhland's poems; Wildenbruch's *Das edle Blut.*

4. The work of the fourth year should comprise the reading of about five hundred pages of good literature in prose and poetry, reference readings upon the lives and works of the great writers studied, the writing in German of numerous short themes upon assigned subjects, independent translation of English into German.

Spanish (2 units).

In Spanish the commission adopts the definitions of the two units of the College Entrance Examination Board, which are in close harmony with the definitions of French and German of the Modern Language Association.

1. During the first year the work should comprise (1) careful drill in pronunciation; (2) the rudiments of grammar, including the conjugation of the regular and the more common irregular verbs, the inflection of nouns, adjectives and pronouns, and the elementary rules of syntax; (3) exercises containing illustrations of the principles of grammar; (4) the reading and accurate rendering into good English of from 100 to 175 duodecimo pages of graduated texts, with translation into Spanish of easy variations of the sentences read; (5) writing Spanish from dictation.

2. During the second year the work should comprise: (1) the reading of from 250 to 400 pages of modern prose from different authors; (2) practice in translating Spanish into English, and English variations of the text into Spanish; (3) continued study of the elements of grammar and syntax; (4) mastery of all but the rare

irregular verb forms and of the simpler uses of the modes and tenses; (5) writing Spanish from dictation; (6) memorizing of easy short poems.

Suitable texts for the second year are: Valera's *El pajaro verde;* Alarcon's *El final de Norma;* Valdes's *José;* Galdos's *Dona Perfecta, Marianela;* Padre Isla's version of *Gil Blas;* Carrion and Aza's *Zaragueta.*

Physics (1 unit).

It is recommended that the candidate's preparation in physics should include:

(*a*) Individual laboratory work, comprising at least thirty-five exercises selected from a list of sixty or more, not very different from the list given below.

(*b*) Instruction by lecture-table demonstrations, to be used mainly as a basis for questioning upon the general principles involved in the pupil's laboratory investigations.

(*c*) The study of at least one standard text-book, supplemented by the use of many and varied numerical problems, to the end that a pupil may gain a correct and comprehensive view of the method of physical science.

FIRST PART.

*Mechanics and Hydrostatics—*Weight of unit volume of a substance; Lifting effect of water upon a body entirely immersed in it; Specific gravity of a solid body that will sink in water; Specific gravity of a block of wood by use of a sinker; Weight of water displaced by a floating body; Specific gravity by flotation method; Specific gravity of a liquid (two methods); The straight lever: first class; Center of gravity and weight of a lever; Levers of the second and third classes; Force exerted at the fulcrum of a lever; Errors of a spring balance; Parallelogram of forces; Friction between solid bodies (on a level); Coefficient of friction (by sliding on incline).

Light—Use of photometer; Images in a plane mirror; Images formed by a convex cylindrical mirror; Images formed by a concave cylindrical mirror; Index of refraction of glass; Index of refraction of water; Focal length of a converging lens; Conjugate foci of a lens; Shape and size of a real image formed by a lens; Virtual image formed by a lens.

SECOND PART.

Mechanics—Breaking-strength of a wire; Comparisons of wires in breaking tests; Elasticity: stretching; Elasticity: bending; effect of varying loads; Elasticity: bending; effect of varying dimensions; Elasticity: twisting; Specific gravity of a liquid by balancing columns; Compressibility of air: Boyle's law; Density of air; Four forces at right angles in one plane; Comparison of masses by acceleration test; Action and reaction; elastic collision, Elastic collision continued: inelastic collision.

Heat—Testing a mercury thermometer; Linear expansion of a solid; Increase of pressure of a gas heated at constant volume; Increase of volume of a gas heated at constant pressure; Specific heat of a solid; Latent heat of melting; Determination of the dew-point; Latent heat of vaporization.

Sound—Velocity of sound; Wave-length of sound; Number of vibrations of a tuning-fork.

Electricity and Magnetism—Lines of force near a bar magnet; Study of a single-fluid galvanic cell; Study of a two-fluid galvanic cell; Lines of force about a galvanoscope; Resistance of wires by substitution: various lengths; Resistance of wires by substitution: cross-section and multiple arc; Resistance by Wheatstone's bridge; Specific resistance of copper; Temperature-coefficient of resistance in copper; Battery resistance; Putting together the parts of a telegraph key and sounder; Putting together the parts of a small motor; Putting together the parts of a small dynamo.

Chemistry (1 unit).

Chemistry is an art as well as a science. Acquaintance with its elements includes ability to *do* certain things *intelligently* as well as remembrance of the bare results of chemical changes. An organized account of the latter is only a sort of dessicated residuum if it is not illuminated by the experience acquired along with skill in the former. The books usually—and necessarily—give prominence to the second (the systematic aspect), leaving instruction in the art to the teacher. A requirement in chemistry, on the other hand, must emphasize the art, for it is universal. It will lay less stress on any particular list of substances, reactions, or topics, in view of the extent of the available material, the briefness of the school course and the consequent differences between equally good individual selections. The art cannot, of course, be acquired without a fair systematic knowledge, while a semblance of the systematic knowledge may be acquired without the art. The art is therefore more worthy of emphasis.

It will be noted that the art of chemistry consists in the practical knowledge of the physical properties of all kinds of matter and the utilization of this knowledge in arranging intelligently the conditions before chemical change, in noting all physical indications during experiment and distinguishing the significant ones, and in interpreting the result of this observation. It thus deals almost exclusively with physical conceptions and facts. It demands, therefore, a careful training in physical facts, physical observation and physical inference. Conventionalized chemical work which can progress without skill in this art (for example, reiterated observation of precipitations) is valueless.

Disregarding questions of order, and simply classifying the essential principles of instruction, the pupil should be taught:

1. *Technique of experimentation.*

    Properties of common apparatus in respect to structure and material. For example, how to make an apparatus air-tight and why. Object of such operations as washing and drying gases and how the object is attained.

    Physical properties which may be used for recognition of each substance and for explanation of all observations.

    Judicious use of proportions and materials. Influence of conditions (temperature, homogeneous and heterogeneous mixture, etc.) on chemical change.

2. Physical phenomena, their recognition, description, and physical interpretation.

3. The more strictly *chemical application* of the results. For example, inference in regard to the nature of the chemical change which must have led to the results observed. Making of the chemical equation from adequate data.

The material basis for the above may be found for the most part in the employment of a restricted number of elements and a few of their chief compounds. Facts should be simplified and systematized by generalization, and generalizations ("laws") should be illustrated and applied to familiar things. The usual theoretical explanations should be given as the facts accumulate. Laws and theories derive their importance from the facts, not *vice versa,* and none should be given unless and until the corresponding facts have been encountered in laboratory or class-room experiments.

A knowledge of important chemical industries and ability to work simple problems will be expected.

The teacher is referred for a list of suitable topics to the Report of the N. E. A. Committee on College Entrance Requirements, or the entrance requirements of the College Entrance Board of the Middle States and Maryland. Many existing text-books cover the same ground.

Detailed discussion of the aims to be kept in view and the methods to be used in instruction will be found in Smith and Hall, *The Teaching of Chemistry and Physics in the Secondary School* (New York: Longmans, Green & Co.).

Physical Geography (1 unit).

The following outline includes only the most essential facts and principles of physical geography, which must be studied in the class room and laboratory:

The Earth as a Globe.

> Shape of earth, how proved, consequences of shape.
> Size: how earth is measured; effects of size.
> Rotation: character of motion; latitude, longitude and time.
> Revolution: rate, path, direction and the consequences.
> Magnetism: compass, poles, variation.
> Map projection.

The Ocean.

> Form, divisions, and general characteristics of the ocean.
> Depth, density, temperature of ocean waters.
> Characteristics of ocean floor.
> Distribution of life in oceans.
> Movement of ocean waters.
>> Waves—Cause and effect.
>> Currents—causes, proofs of causes, important currents, effect of currents.

Tides—character of motion, cause of tides, variation of tides, bores.

Work of Ocean.

Classes of shore lines and importance of shore lines.

The Atmosphere.

Composition and offices of atmosphere.

Instruments used in study of atmosphere.

Temperature.

Source and variation of atmospheric temperatures.

Isothermal charts of world, January and July, with special study of isotherms of northern and southern hemispheres, of location of heat equator, of cold pole, of crowded isotherms, etc.

Pressure.

Measurement of pressure.

Use of pressure in altitude determinations.

Relation to temperature.

Study of isobars on U. S. Weather Map.

Distribution of pressure over world in January and July.

Relation of isobars to isotherms.

Circulation of atmosphere.

Winds, classes, directions, causes, effects.

Moisture.

Source, forms of, measurement of, precipitation.

Storms.

Paths and characters of storms of United States.

Daily weather at different seasons.

Relation of storms to general weather conditions.

Relation of weather to climate.

The Land.

Several features of land as compared with ocean.

Distribution of land.

Map representation of topography.

Changes in land forms, effects of elevation and depression.

Plains.

Kinds of plains.

Characteristics of different kinds.

Development of plains.

Coastal plain of eastern United States in parts.

Alluvial plains, their formation and importance.

Relation of life conditions to different forms of plains.

Plateaus.

Young plateaus.

Dissected plateaus.

Old plateaus.

Broken plateaus.

Mountains.

Block mountains.

Folded mountains.

Domed mountains.

Massive mountains.

Volcanoes.

Distribution.

Character of, at different stages.

Rivers.

Life history of river—work of rivers, topography of valleys at different stages, lake and lake basins.

Revived rivers.

Drowned valleys.

The great drainage basins of the United States.

Glaciers.

Existing ice sheets.

Kinds of glaciers.

Work of glaciers.

Characteristics of glaciated area of northern United States.

Summary.

Relation of man, plants, and animals, to climate, land forms, and oceanic areas.

The outline given can but present the larger topics to be covered, and in a way to suggest the point of view desired. Each topic should be treated so as to show its causal relations to other topics, and, so far as possible, the effects of earth features on life conditions should be emphasized.

The candidate's preparation should include:

a. The study of one of the leading secondary text books in physical geography, that a knowlege may be gained of the essential principles, and of well-selected facts illustrating those principles.

b. Individual laboratory work, comprising at least forty exercises. From one-third to one-half of the candidate's class-room work should be devoted to laboratory exercises. In the autumn and spring, field trips should take the place of laboratory exercises.

Botany (1 unit).

The following course is designed to include those topics in the leading divisions of the subject which are now regarded by most teachers as fundamental. Individual laboratory work by the student is essential, and should receive at least double the amount of time given to recitation.

The full year's course consists of two parts:

Part I. The general principles of (a) *Anatomy and Morphology,* (b) *Physiology and* (c) *Ecology.*

a. *In Anatomy and Morphology.*

The Seed. Four types (dicotyledon without and with endosperm, a monocotyledon and a gymnosperm); structure and homologous parts. Food supply; experimental determination of its nature and value. Phenomena of germination and growth of embryo into a seedling (including bursting from the seed, assumption of position and unfolding of parts).

The Shoot. Gross anatomy of a typical shoot, including the relationships of position of leaf, stem (and root), the arrangement of leaves and buds on the stem, and deviations (through light adjustment, etc.) from symmetry. Buds, and the mode of origin of new leaf and stem; winter buds in particular.

Specialized and metamorphosed shoots (stems and leaves). General structure and distribution of the leading tissues of the shoot; annual growth; shedding of bark and leaves.

The Root. Gross anatomy of a typical root; position and origin of secondary roots; hair-zone, cap and growing point.

Specialized and metamorphosed roots. General structure and distribution of the leading tissues of the root.

The Flower. Structure of a typical flower, especially of ovule and pollen; functions of the parts.

Comparative morphological study of six or more different marked types, with the construction of transverse and longitudinal diagrams.

The Fruit. Structure of a typical fruit, especially with reference to changes from the flower, and from ovule to seed. Comparative morphological study of six or more marked types, with diagrams.

The Cell. Cytoplasm, Nucleus, Sap-cavity, Wall. Adaptive modifications of walls, formation of tissues.

b. *In Physiology.*

Role of water in the plant; *absorption (osmosis), path of transfer, transpiration, turgidity and its mechanical value, plasmolysis.*

Photosynthesis; *dependence of starch formation upon chlorophyll, light and carbon dioxide; evolution of oxygen,* observation of starch grains.

Respiration; *necessity for oxygen in growth, evolution of carbon dioxide.*

Digestion; *digestion of starch with diastase,* and its role in translocation of foods.

Irritability; *Geotropism, heliotropism and hydrotropism;* nature of stimulus and response.

Growth; *localization in higher plants; amount in germinating seeds and stems; relationships to temperature.*

Fertilization; sexual and vegetative reproduction.

c. *In Ecology.*

Modifications (metamorphoses) of parts for special functions.

Dissemination.

Cross-pollination.

Light relations of green tissues; leaf mosaics.

Plant Societies; Mesophytes, Hydrophytes, Halophytes, Xerophytes; Climbers, Epiphytes, Parasites (and Saprophytes), Insectivora.

Plant Associations, and zonal distribution.

Part II. The Natural History of the Plant Groups, and Classification.

A comprehensive summary of the great natural groups of plants, based upon the thorough study of the structure, reproduction and adaptations to a habitat of one or two types from each group, supplemented and extended by more rapid study of other forms in those groups. Where living material is wanting for the latter, preserved material and even good pictures may be used, and a standard text-book should be thoroughly read. The general homologies from group to group should be noted.

In general in this part of the course much less attention should be given to the lower and inconspicuous groups, and progressively more to the higher and conspicuous forms.

Following is a list of recommended types from which, or their equivalents, selection may be made:

a *Algae*, Pleurococcus, Sphærella, Spirogyra, Vaucheria, Fucus, Nemalion (or Polysiphonia or Coleochæte).

b. *Fungi*. Bacteria, Mucor, Yeast, Puccinia (or any Powdery Mildew), Mushroom.

c. *Lichens*, Physcia (or Parmelia).

d. *Byrophytes*. In Hepaticæ, Radula or Porella or Marchantia). In Musci; Mnium (or Funaria or Polytrichum).

e. *Pteridophytes*. In Filicineae, Aspidium or equivalent, including, of course, the prothallus.
In Equesetineæ, Equisetum.
In Lycopodineæ, Lycopolidum and Selaginella (or Isoetes).

f. *Gymnosperms*. Pinus or equivalent.

g. *Angiosperms*. A monocotyledon and a dicotyledon, to be studied with reference to the homologies of their parts with those in the above groups; together with representative plants of the leading subdivisions and principal families of Angiosperms.

Classification should include a study of the primary subdivisions of the above groups, based on the comparison of the types with other (preferably) living or preserved material. The principal subdivisions of the Angiosperms, grouped on the Engler and Prantl system, should be understood.

Biology (1 unit).

a. Work in botany as defined above, to the amount of one-half a unit.

b. Zoology: The study of not to exceed ten type forms.

The line of study to be followed for each form is indicated by the following analysis:

1. External anatomy: (1) General form and symmetry, regions, parts; (2) comparison with other individuals of the same species, emphasizing points of variation and constancy; (3) comparison with other types.

2. Observations on the living animal, simple physiological tests, emphasizing care with regard to the inferences drawn from the reactions.

3. Class topics, including talks by the teacher, selected readings, class work, analysis with results.

As a specific instance of the application to the individual form, the following is taken from the report of a member of the committee on zoology of the Department of Science of the N. E. A.:

BUTTERFLY.

Any one of various species whose larvæ can be obtained alive near the end of September may be employed. The cabbage butterfly (Pieris), the milkweed butterfly (Danais), or the swallow-tail butterfly (Papilio) will meet these conditions.

DRAWINGS.

1. Imago: dorsal view, wings expanded. X, 1 or 2.
2. Imago: left side, wings closed. (The bodies in 1 and 2 are to be drawn parallel to each other). X, 1 or 2.
3. Imago: front of head. X, 10.
4. Pupa: left side.
5. Full-grown larva: dorsal view.
6. Full-grown larva: left side.

QUESTIONS OF EXTERNAL ANATOMY.

1. How many segments behind the head in (*a*) the imago; (*b*) the larva; (*c*) the pupa?
2. What external organs of the imago can be identified in the pupa?
3. Which feet of the larva correspond with those of the imago?

OBSERVATIONS ON THE LIVING LARVA.

Each student (or group of students) should be provided with a glass vessel covered with netting and containing food leaves, for keeping the larva during pupation.

1. How is locomotion effected? Illustrate by diagrams.
2. How does the larva feed? Observe and record the movements of the mouthparts and of the head during feeding. Draw the outline of a partly eaten leaf.
3. (This observation must extend through several days.) Make and record observations upon the act of pupation.

TOPICS FOR THE TEACHER.

(1) The habits and food of butterflies. (2) The number of broods of butterflies during a single season and seasonal dimorphism. (3) Protective resemblance and mimicry. (4) The larger divisions and commoner native forms of lepidoptera. (Examples of lepidoptera illustrating the commoner native types should be shown, and stu-

dents encouraged to collect and classify them.) (5) The hymenoptera; their structure, classification, and habits.

In physics, chemistry, physical geography, botany, and biology the definitions are based on the recommendation of the Science Department of the N. E. A. and the requirements of the College Entrance Examination Board.

RECOMMENDATIONS OF THE SUB-COMMITTEE ON HIGH SCHOOL INSPECTION.

To the Commission on Accredited Schools:

Gentlemen: Your committee to whom was assigned for consideration the "steps necessary to secure uniformity in the standards and methods, and economy of labor and expense in the work of high school inspection," and also the "preparation of a list of high schools within the territory of this Association which are entitled to this accredited relationship," begs leave to report that it held a somewhat extended meeting in Chicago the day following the final adjournment of the Commission, deliberated upon the same as carefully as the time at its disposal and the importance of the subjects would admit, and offers the following as a result of its reflections:

I. As to standards. Your committee believes that the basal factor in any plan looking toward a reasonably uniform system of accredited schools is necessarily the course of study; but as the consideration of this problem has been referred to another committee, it has omitted it from its deliberations. Your committee has deemed it appropriate, however, to make certain recommendations concerning the standards of organization, teaching force, equipment, general efficiency, etc., required of schools admitted to the general list of accredited schools, and therefore submits the following:

1. That the minimum scholastic attainment of all high school teachers be the equivalent of graduation from a college belonging to the North Central Association of Colleges and Secondary Schools, including special training in the subjects they teach, although such requirement shall not be construed as retroactive.

Your committee believes that the efficiency of the average college or university graduate is very materially enhanced by professional study, observation, and training in practice teaching under skilled supervision, and therefore advises that the accredited schools be urged to give due preference to teachers possessing such preparation.

2. Your committee advises that the number of daily periods of class-room instruction given by any one teacher should not exceed five, each to extend over a period of forty-five minutes.

3. That the laboratory and library facilities be adequate to the needs of instruction in the subjects taught as outlined in the report of the Commission.

4. That while the foregoing are exceedingly important factors affecting the quality of the work, the *esprit de corps,* the efficiency of the instruction, the acquired habits of thought and study, and the general intellectual and ethical tone of the school are of paramount importance, and therefore only schools which rank well in these particulars, as evidenced by rigid, thorough-going, sympathetic inspection, should be considered eligible to the list.

II. As to inspection. Your committee recommends that a board of five inspectors be appointed to ascertain the schools within the territory of the North Central Association entitled to the accredited relationship under the above limitations.

III. To facilitate the work of the board of inspectors in the preparation and submission of a list of high schools justly entitled to this accredited relationship, your committee recommends:

1. That the Commission cause to be printed and distributed to the several inspectors of the colleges and universities of the North Central Association the following uniform blanks:

a. Principal's blank form for report relative to organization, teaching force, attendance, library, laboratory, etc. This report should be filled and returned to the inspector not later than November 1 of each year.

b. Inspector's blank forms for report of examination of each school.

c. Student's blank forms for recommendation to colleges and universities.

2. That it shall be the duty of the board of inspectors to submit to the secretary of the Commission the list of schools recommended by them as entitled to this relationship not later than June 1 of each year.

3. That it shall be the duty of the secretary of this Commission to publish the list submitted to him by the board of inspectors not later than June 10 of each year, and to cause the same to be distributed to the members of the North Central Association.

The committee believes that this list of schools should be an honor list for the North Central States, and, for that reason, has made specific recommendations with reference to requirements in the matter of organization, equipment, teaching force, and standards of scholarship. When once this system has been thoroughly organized and systematized, it may be found practicable to extend the privileges of accredited relationship to smaller schools, but the committee recommends that nothing less than the standards herein recommended shall be deemed acceptable in the beginning. The Commission on Accredited Schools has an opportunity to assist immeasurably in strengthening secondary education in the Northwest, and the committee believes that this will be best accomplished by starting with a comparatively select list of schools.

Furthermore, your committee believes that the Commission should refrain from any action which will lead to standardization of secondary schools and methods of inspection. It is our belief that the cause of secondary education will be best advanced by a somewhat free and natural development in the several states.

Respectfully submitted for the committee,

A. S. WHITNEY,
Chairman.

CPSIA information can be obtained
at www.ICGtesting.com
Printed in the USA
BVHW040912050219
539516BV00009B/267/P